Company
Law and
Competition

Mergers, Acquisitions and Alternative Corporate Strategies
Hill Samuel Bank Limited

Tax: Strategic Corporate Tax Planning
Price Waterhouse

Finance for Growth
National Westminster Bank PLC

Company Law and Competition
S J Berwin & Co

Marketing: Communicating with the Consumer
D'Arcy Masius Benton & Bowles

Information Technology: The Catalyst for Change
PA Consulting Group

Marketing to the Public Sector and Industry
Rank Xerox Limited

Transport and Distribution
TNT Express

Property
Edward Erdman Surveyors

Employment and Training
Blue Arrow PLC

Company Law and Competition

S J Berwin & Co

With a Foreword by
Sir Leon Brittan, QC
Vice-President of the Commission of the European Communities

Published in association with
CBI Initiative 1992

MERCURY BOOKS
Published by W.H. Allen & Co. Plc

First published in 1989
by the Mercury Books Division of
W.H. Allen & Co. Plc
Sekforde House, 175–9 St John Street, London EC1V 4LL

Set in Plantin by Phoenix Photosetting, Chatham
Printed and bound in Great Britain by
Mackays of Chatham PLC, Letchworth, Herts

British Library Cataloguing in Publication Data

Company law and competition
   1. European Community countries. Companies.
European Economic Community law
I. SJ Berwin & Co   II. Confederation of
British Industry
341.7'53

ISBN 1–85251–027–7

Contents

Foreword

As 1992 approaches, businesses throughout the European Community are gearing themselves up to face new challenges and grasp new opportunities. A transformation is taking place as companies adapt to new conditions and to the emerging reality of a single market of 320 million consumers.

This process of adaptation, which is already well under way, is essential to the completion of the single market. It is the task of the Community institutions to provide the right environment for market integration. This involves a range of activities from the creation of a common legislative framework – not least in the area of company law – to the mutual recognition of standards and qualifications. However, ultimately it is European business itself which, through its response to the new, barrier-free environment, will transform the single market into reality.

As Commissioner with responsibility for competition policy – a subject which is of particular interest to businesses looking at expanding opportunities in Europe – I should like to emphasise the importance which the Commission places upon maintaining open, competitive markets within the Community. The effective implementation of the existing EC competition rules has already made an important contribution to the creation of a genuine single market. Indeed, together with the legal provisions which prevent the imposition of regulatory barriers to the free movement of goods, the Community's competition policy is one of the foundation stones of the internal market structure. The fact that companies may not restrict or distort competition in intra-Community trade helps them to adopt a positive attitude towards operating within Europe – looking outwards rather than inwards, and seeking expansion rather than protection. As such it contributes to preparing the ground for 1992 and for the wider challenges of world markets.

Competition policy will be equally, if not more, important in the future. This has been fully recognised by the Cecchini Report, which emphasised that the benefits of market integration would be achieved only in a dynamic competitive economic environment where new market barriers are not erected in place of those which have been dismantled. Concentrations of economic power which lead to market dominance and reduce or eliminate competition must be dealt with at Community level. At the same time, legal certainty must be provided for companies whose plans for expansion or co-operative ventures do not lead to adverse effects on competition. Such plans are, after all, a reflection of the successful development of the single market.

In concluding, it is worth observing that in this vital, formative period of the single market, companies must have adequate *information*. In order to maximise their prospects in an economically integrated Europe, they must *know* about the present legal position, the changes which have taken place and the developments which are likely to occur in the foreseeable future. Company law and competition policy are two fields in which such information is particularly important. I have been greatly encouraged by recent signs that business is alive to the possibilities and is responding to the challenges. This book and the associated CBI Initiative 1992 fully illustrate my point. I congratulate S J Berwin & Co on all they have done to promote this important initiative, and it gives me particular pleasure to have been invited to support them.

Sir Leon Brittan, QC
Vice-President of the Commission of the European Communities

Preface

In 1974, in one of the first cases to come before the English courts in which questions of Community law were raised, Lord Denning described the implications of Community law for the English legal system as 'an incoming tide. It flows into the estuaries and up the rivers. It cannot be held back.'

The impact of Community law on our own domestic laws since then and the sheer scope of its subject matter, in particular since the launch in 1985 of the Commission's White Paper 'Completing the internal market', suggests that even Lord Denning may not have foreseen the full force of the oncoming tide of Community law. Few areas of legal activity are now untouched by Community law and UK businesses that fail to take account of its implications as part of their 1992 business strategy planning do so at their peril.

This book, prepared as part of the CBI's Initiative 1992, endeavours to explain and describe in non-technical terms the Community laws on company law and competition. Company law and competition were selected from the diverse and wide spectrum of Community legal activity because of their general importance to all sectors of UK industry in the lead-up to 1992. Together they establish the general rules for growth of UK businesses both organically and in partnership with Community counterparts and provide essential checks and balances so that a spirit of open and free competition will regulate the many changes to which UK businesses must adapt as 1992 approaches. Consideration is given not only to company law strictly so-called but also to Community measures relating to the right of establishment and the provision of services and, in particular, to the harmonisation of national rules regulating specific business activities. In addition to outlining the general application of EC competition rules, we examine their specific application to a number of legal scenarios of particular relevance to business executives in their 1992 strategy planning.

This book is written first and foremost for business executives rather than for lawyers. It endeavours to distil this legally complex subject matter into a form which we hope makes it accessible to those business executives and non-EC law specialists to whom CBI Initiative 1992 is principally addressed.

A significant role in the preparation and writing of this book was played by Derrick Wyatt, Fellow of St Edmund Hall, Oxford, barrister. We are indebted to him for all his assistance and encouragement. We are extremely grateful to leading firms of lawyers, Rycken Burlion Bolle & Houben in Belgium, Gide Loyrette Nouel in France, Modest Gundisch Landry in West Germany, Gomez-Acebo & Pombo in Spain and Studio Legale Bisconti in Italy, for their advice on those parts of this book which refer to their domestic laws and in particular for their contributions to the Case Study on pp. 166–82. We are also most grateful to Bill Belcher for his cartoons which appear throughout this book.

This book deals with the law in force on 1 January 1989, except where later developments are specifically mentioned.

By its very nature, this book is not intended to be a full statement of the law, either in general or in its application to particular situations or transactions. Those considering the EC aspects of any situation or transaction should seek competent professional advice at that time, for which this book does not pretend to be a substitute.

I
Company law and business regulation in the context of the single market

1.   Introduction

The single market

One of the main tasks of the EC is to assimilate commercial activities in and between the twelve member states to commercial activities within a single state. Thus, for example, customs duties, discriminatory internal taxation and quotas have been abolished. Companies are given the right to sell their goods and services across national frontiers, and to set up agencies and branches in other member states. To facilitate this, many aspects of national company law have been 'harmonised', that is to say made uniform, by Community rules. Proposals are also in train to establish a European corporate framework to operate independently of the various national systems.

Since one of the principal objects of this single market is to promote competition, restrictive trading agreements and unfair monopolistic practices are prohibited by the Treaty of Rome and Community regulations. The borderline between permissible co-operation on the one hand, and impermissible restrictive practices on the other, may be a fine one, and it is important that companies remain abreast of legal developments in this area. They will be anxious to avoid the stiff sanctions of the EC competition rules, and may themselves wish to invoke the rules against anti-competitive practices on the part of other companies. The Commission is charged with the task of enforcing the competition rules, and enjoys discretionary powers to exempt agreements which, despite containing certain clauses which restrict competition, have the overall effect of promoting economic progress and benefiting consumers. The process of completing the internal market is not over. Great advances have already been made towards the achievement of a Europe without internal frontiers on the target date of 31 December 1992, but even that date will not signal the end of the road. For the process of 'neutralising' the effect of national laws and practices on trade between member states must continually adapt to changing economic and political conditions in the Community. UK companies are able to influence the content of the evolving Community rules through their representative institutions, which in turn exert an influence on the Council, Commission and European Parliament.

Opportunities and risks

The development of the single market poses a challenge, which has no parallel in peacetime this century, to the resourcefulness of UK industry. It provides the opportunity to exploit a 'home market' comparable in scale to that of the USA. Yet competing successfully in Europe means competing according to Community rules. This is so even if a company fails to export to Europe a single nut, bolt, software package or policy of insurance. For the rules apply throughout the Community, and many of the company law and competition rules apply irrespective of whether or not a company is engaged in inter-state transactions. It is probably obvious that Community law applies when a stock exchange listing is sought in another member state, or a distributorship arrangement or joint venture is contemplated in another member state. Yet Community law equally applies when a UK company is seeking a listing in the UK, or contemplating a takeover in the UK, or considering a joint venture or distributorship in the UK. It has never before been more important to incorporate informed legal advice into corporate decision making. Businesses cannot afford to ignore the European legal framework. Infringement of European rules may lead to substantial fines and adverse publicity. And it can be equally damaging if unfamiliarity with Community mechanisms leaves an enterprise exposed to anti-competitive practices where effective remedies lie readily to hand if the proper advice is sought.

Law making at European level

The grand design of a single market for Europe requires more than free trade guarantees in the founding Treaties. It requires that the political institutions of the Community – the Council, Commission and Parliament – co-operate in the making of legislation to meet the demands of the evolving European market. The Treaty of Rome has always provided for weighted majority voting on a number of issues, including competition law and company law. Until recently, however, a political understanding – 'the Luxembourg compromise' – allowed member states to 'veto' European legislation adversely affecting their vital national interests. The Single European Act, which came into force in July 1987, made important amendments to the Treaty of Rome. Legislative decisions on most issues can now be taken by weighted majority, if put to the vote, though in certain matters, such as tax harmonisation or the legal rights of employees, the Treaty of Rome requires unanimity.

Single European Act

**European
Parliament**

The Single European Act also increased the powers of the European Parliament. In particular, the rejection by the European Parliament of a Commission proposal to the Council can prevent a decision being taken by a weighted ('qualified') majority, and necessitate a unanimous vote. The European Parliament now also has to approve association agreements with countries outside the EC, and recently made news by delaying agreement with Israel.

More than ever before, it is essential that UK businesses make their views on European legal proposals felt, not only at national level, but at the level of Commission and Parliament – especially where the possibility exists that legislation might take effect by qualified majority.

European Court

Since a measure's basis in the Treaty of Rome can influence the voting rules to be applied in the Council, legal disputes on such matters may call for resolution by the European Court. For example, in 1985 the Council adopted a particular Directive by a qualified majority; the UK voted against it. The Directive concerned the use in livestock farming of certain substances having a hormonal action. It was based on the Treaty of Rome's provisions governing the Common Agricultural Policy, which requires only a qualified majority. The UK took the view that it should have been based on Article 100 of the Treaty of Rome, which requires unanimity, in which case the adverse vote of the UK could have prevented the Directive being adopted. The UK challenged the Directive in the European Court, but the Court accepted that the agricultural policy provisions of the Treaty of Rome provided an adequate basis for the Directive. The episode illustrates beyond doubt that the majority voting rules of the Treaty of Rome have teeth.

There is no better example of the potential significance of voting structures for UK business than the company law harmonisation programme. Community measures based on Articles 54(3)(g) and 57(2) may under those provisions be passed on the basis of a qualified majority vote in the Council, subject to resort to the 'Luxembourg compromise'. Thus the Fifth Company Law Directive (contentious for its provisions on employee representation at board level) could be passed by a qualified majority. It is an open question whether the political understanding allowing member states claiming a vital national interest to avoid application of the formal voting rules could be successfully invoked to enable a member state to 'veto' such a decision. Measures based on Article 100 require unanimity. Article 100A of the Treaty of Rome (as introduced by the Single European Act) allows qualified majority voting by way of derogation from Article 100, but Article 100A does not apply to the free movement of persons, which under the Treaty of Rome includes the right of corporate establishment, or to the rights of employed persons (and so, for example, the Vredeling Directive can only be passed under Article 100 by unanimity, since it is principally concerned with the rights of employed persons, and thus cannot be based upon Articles 54, 57 or 100A).

Call this a level playing-field?

Influencing Community legislation

Lobbying

Since the Community institutions make law, and since industry has a legitimate interest in the content of that law, UK lobbying is no longer confined to Westminster and Whitehall. Since the powers of the European Parliament were enhanced by the Single European Act in July 1987, lobbying of MEPs and the European Parliament's committees has taken on new significance. Especially where company law is concerned, the consultative role of the Economic and Social Committee gives UK businesses an opportunity, through the CBI, of influencing Community legislation. However, under the Community's legislative procedures, it is the Commission which plays the most important role. It both proposes legislation and has to decide (subject to any final decision by the Council) whether to accept any amendment put forward by the European Parliament. In determining its position at any stage of the legislative process, and particularly when the proposal is still in draft, the Commission may be influenced by reasoned argument and a factual analysis by the business community. Arguments designed to influence legislation should be presented in a balanced and non-doctrinaire way. In dealing with the Commission, it is helpful if businesses know which Directorate-General of the Commission deals with the matter in question, and which is the responsible government department in the UK. It is not uncommon for the same Commission officials concerned with proposing draft legislation to be responsible for the enforcement of that legislation against member states when it is passed. This makes a working relationship with Commission officials and appreciation of their approach to legal problems of particular value to businesses.

The same kind of links which have been established over the years between law firms and business on the one hand, and UK government departments on the other, must be forged with European institutions. A good working relationship with Commission officials has thus become a high priority for those law firms which offer advice on Community law to UK businesses. A phone call to a particular official in the Commission can yield faster results than a written inquiry to a Directorate-General – and time is money.

Legal advice on European matters

Progress towards the single market provides as much of a challenge to legal advisers as it does to their clients. For a commercial firm of solicitors, expertise in Community law does not simply grow like Topsy. It requires a conscious policy decision to treat Community law as part and parcel of the legal framework in which day-to-day legal advice is offered to business clients. Offering advice on Community law involves recruiting specialists, providing continuing legal education on Community law to lawyers in all departments, and equipping library and information centres with all relevant Community documentation.

For lawyers it is especially important to establish contact with colleagues in other member states. Many business decisions require input from lawyers in several member states, who can advise on the inter-relationship between their national rules and the Community rules. Technology can provide vital assistance in the provision of informed legal advice. Familiarity with multilingual legal databases can provide up-to-date information not only on current legal rules but also on the course of legislation proposed by the Commission and currently pending before the Parliament or the Council. It is for lawyers to make a reality of the single market for UK enterprises, wherever in the Community they choose to locate their business activities, or to sell their goods and services.

2. Impact and scope of the single market

Opportunities in the single market

As the single market develops, it will progressively integrate the distinct national markets which have for so long characterised trade in Europe. The single market will provide opportunities for growth on the basis of the quality and reliability of goods and services irrespective of the location of producer, supplier, wholesaler, retailer or customer. Yet this will not mean that the whole of Europe will beat its way to the door of UK business. Opportunities will exist that did not exist before, but it will be for companies to make the most of those opportunities. If they do not, they cannot expect to thrive in the new commercial and legal environment. The following sections explain the scope of the single market and how its attainment will provide opportunities for growth.

Traditional barriers to trade in Europe

Before the establishment of the Common Market in 1957 the different national markets were separated by barriers of three distinct kinds:

- Barriers erected by the member states themselves for the purpose of isolating the national markets and protecting domestic industries (for example, customs duties, quotas, state monopolies, discriminatory taxes and other discriminatory measures, and state subsidies to local industries).

- Barriers resulting from the disparities between national legal systems. Thus, for example, the different licensing systems in the different member states inhibited the provision of financial services across state lines; and the different systems of company law could make joint ventures and mergers costly and complicated.

- Barriers arising from the restrictive practices and cartels of business enterprises. Agreements to collaborate rather than to compete could have the effect of reinforcing a partitioning of national markets underpinned by national customs duties, exchange controls and quotas. A similar isolation of national markets could result from the abusive and predatory practices of businesses which by virtue of their market share and technical and financial resources enjoyed dominant positions on those national markets.

Dismantling the barriers

The Treaty of Rome and the Single European Act, which amends it and seeks to accelerate progress towards a single market in 1992, commit the member states to dismantle their traditional barriers.

Tariffs and quotas

Tariffs, quotas and internal barriers are comprehensively regulated by the Treaty of Rome and by legislation made by the Commission and Council. It is in this field that the single market is most advanced. For example, apart from narrowly interpreted exceptions which may be invoked by member states in their national interests, customs duties and quotas on imports from other member states and discriminatory internal taxes are absolutely prohibited, as are discriminatory national measures capable of inhibiting the freedom of establishment of companies and their freedom to provide services across national frontiers without the establishment of agencies, branches or subsidiaries. (Transitional provisions still apply to Spain and Portugal.) This impressive achievement has provided enormous opportunities for any EC company to find new markets for its goods and services in the territories of other member states.

Establishment, services and company law harmonisation

A single market cannot be said to exist unless companies incorporated in one member state are permitted to do business in another. In practical terms, business across national frontiers may be conducted in several ways. A UK company may set up an agency, branch or subsidiary in another member state, and carry on its business through

Establishment

Provision of services

that local office. This form of doing business is known as 'establishment'. Investment in an agency, branch or subsidiary will be expected to pay for itself by generating extra business. This may not be possible in the short term, and initially a UK company may prefer to make sales and win clients in another EC market without the benefit of a local office, and through the activities of visiting marketing personnel or intermediaries. This simpler form of doing business is known as the 'provision of services' – whether the object of the exercise is in fact the provision of services (for example, giving investment advice) or the marketing of goods.

This book is largely concerned with the implications for businesses of the removal of such barriers to trade in Europe, which by their nature cannot simply be prohibited. What is needed are evolving Community policies in the fields of company law, business regulation and competition, which will enable businesses in all the member states to extend their business activities throughout the single market without regard to national frontiers. The principal company law and business regulation aspects of this process are examined later (see pp. 27–48). Companies must be able to provide goods or services across state lines without setting up agencies, branches or subsidiaries where this would be superfluous, and without being subjected to more burdensome rules in the host state than are absolutely necessary. Companies must also be entitled to establish agencies, branches or subsidiaries in other member states, without discrimination on grounds of nationality. Developing Community rules will make it possible to comply with requirements in such areas as company law, securities listing, and insider dealing, that are either uniform in the different member states, or at any rate are regarded as being equivalent, instead of complying with a variety of different rules in different member states. Finally, it will be possible for companies to co-operate with each other within the framework of new corporate forms – such as the European Economic Interest Grouping (EEIG) and the European Company (should that Proposal be adopted) – based upon Community law rather than national law. As these tools are placed in the hands of Europe's businesses, economic activity within the twelve member states will progressively be assimilated to economic activity within a single state. The opportunities for growth in the new and evolving market will be there for all those with the energy and foresight to grasp them.

An integral part of the removal of barriers between member states is the implementation of the fundamental principle of Community law that member states should not discriminate against one another and should assimilate the treatment they accord to nationals from other member states to the treatment they accord to their own nationals. We describe below the practical application of this principle for establishment and the provision of services within the Community.

Equality of treatment for establishment

Abolition of discriminatory rules

Entry into the Common Market brought immediate changes in the terms of national legislation discriminating against foreign companies. For example, the requirement that companies and firms not registered in Denmark obtain prior authorisation from the Ministry of Justice if they wished to acquire land was clearly incompatible with the right of establishment, and could no longer be applied to companies registered in other member states when Denmark joined the EC.

In practice, discriminatory rules may still be encountered in the member states and it is sometimes necessary to invoke EC rules in the appropriate national court in order to secure equal access to the relevant market. The EC rules give EC companies the same rights as

---

Example

In 1983 the City of Biarritz refused to allow a West German artist to tender for municipal premises to be rented for the display of arts and crafts, since the City authorities had decided to restrict the tender to French nationals. The premises in question belonged to the municipal authorities, and they had taken the view that they could let them on whatever conditions they thought fit. The artist brought an action before a French court, which asked for a ruling from the European Court in Luxembourg. The artist won his case. He was entitled to be treated no less favourably than French nationals in the pursuit of his occupation, and this included the right to tender for a lock-up shop in the sought-after Port des Pêcheurs.

---

individuals. It would have made no difference to the above example had the aggrieved party been a West German company with a branch in France tendering for factory space.

The picture is complicated by the fact that national authorities may regard some discrimination between nationals and non-nationals as being necessary in order to ensure the protection of national interests such as the collection of taxes. A recent example illustrates the point. Under the French Tax Code, credits against tax on profits made in France were granted to insurance companies registered in France. However, such tax credits were not granted to agencies or branches of insurance companies which were not registered in France. The Commission regarded this difference of treatment as deterring companies registered in other member states from setting up agencies and branches, since they were placed at a disadvantage *vis-à-vis* French companies. The French authorities said that it was legitimate to differentiate between French companies and non-French companies in order to prevent tax avoidance by the latter. This argument did not satisfy the European Court, which ruled that discriminating between companies on the basis of their corporate nationality would deprive the right of establishment of all meaning. The effect of the Court's judgment was that insurance companies from other member states were free to choose whether to do business in France through an agency or branch on the one hand, or through a subsidiary registered in France on the other, without suffering any tax disadvantages as a result.

Disguised discrimination

National rules sometimes impose conditions on business activity which make no reference to nationality, but nevertheless have the practical effect of discriminating on grounds of nationality. Such rules are compatible with the right of establishment only if any differentiation which results in practice between local companies and companies incorporated in other member states is justifiable. Suppose that national rules of a member state required that the sales managers of all companies marketing products in that state had the appropriate certificate of competence awarded by business schools in that state. This would amount (as the case law of the European Court makes clear) to disguised discrimination, since the sales managers of companies incorporated in other member states would not be likely to have this qualification unless they had been recruited locally. The EC rules on establishment require that in such cases evidence of equivalent expertise acquired in the other member states must be given full faith and credit in the host state.

Sometimes, however, national rules which are in practice more likely to affect out-of-state companies may nevertheless be justifiable if their purpose is consistent with the aims of the single market and any effect on non-national companies is purely incidental. In one case the European Court considered Irish legislation which exempted rural land owned by corporate bodies from compulsory acquisition if all the shareholders had resided for more than one year within three miles of the land. In practice, of course, this condition would rarely be satisfied by foreign companies, or by Irish companies whose shareholders were resident in other member states. However, the European Court accepted that one of the principal purposes of the legislation was to encourage the ownership of rural land by those persons who actually worked it, and that the law was applied equally to nationals and non-nationals alike. The Court concluded that the law was consistent with the EC rules on the right of establishment.

Limits to the right of establishment

The right of establishment can be invoked by a company registered in a member state against the national authorities of that state if they seek to prevent it setting up agencies, branches or subsidiaries, or participating in the incorporation of a company in another member state. However, a company cannot rely upon the right of establishment to transfer its central management and control (broadly, the place where board meetings take place) to another member state. A UK investment company sought to transfer its central management and control to offices in the Netherlands for fiscal reasons, without the consent of the Treasury, which was required under the tax legislation of the UK. Under the law of a number of member states (though not the UK), transfer of central management and control from the state of registration is only possible if the company is wound up and reincorporated in another member state. The European Court held that the existence of such different rules of company law in the member states precluded reliance by the UK company upon the right of establishment to transfer its central management and control to another member state.

Equality of treatment in the provision of services

Abolition of discriminatory rules

From the earliest days of the Community it was recognised that eliminating discrimination on grounds of nationality was as essential for securing the provision of services as it was for establishment. For this reason EC Directives in the 1960s provided for the repeal of such legislation (in so far as it affected nationals of member states) as the requirement of West German law that foreign companies wishing to pursue business activities in West Germany must obtain special authorisation from the West German authorities. Companies formed in the EC are similarly entitled to compete for tenders from public authorities, and to sub-contract work from such authorities, without discrimination on grounds of nationality. They are also eligible under EC rules for any public subsidies available to companies incorporated under the law of the host state.

Disguised discrimination

We have already seen that national rules which do not expressly discriminate on grounds of nationality may nevertheless have this effect in practice.

Example

The Social Insurance Code of Luxembourg provided that temporary workers from outside Luxembourg were exempted from compulsory social insurance, and did not qualify for benefits. Their employers, however, were obliged to pay their share of the social insurance contributions normally payable in respect of such workers in Luxembourg. The reason for this was to prevent temporary foreign labour from undercutting Luxembourg workers. Two French companies, based in France, and specialising in railway maintenance, undertook work in Luxembourg from time to time, using workers who remained affiliated to the French social security institutions. These companies objected to having to pay social security contributions in Luxembourg, in addition to contributions in France, and challenged the Luxembourg rules in a Luxembourg court, which referred the matter to the European Court. The companies argued in the European Court that the practical effect of the rules in question was to place companies incorporated in other member states and doing business temporarily in Luxembourg at a disadvantage compared with local undertakings. The Court agreed. This was indeed disguised discrimination against companies from other member states. The French companies were thereafter relieved of the obligation to pay social insurance contributions in Luxembourg.

Nature of the right of access

Whereas the right of establishment entitles a company incorporated in one member state to set up agencies, branches and subsidiaries, without discrimination on grounds of nationality, in the territory of another, the purpose of the freedom to provide services is to enable a company established in one member state to do business in the territory of another without setting up agencies, branches or subsidiaries, and indeed without complying with all the rules and regulations of the second state, as explained below.

Important consequences flow from this. In the first place, the nationality of the company *vis-à-vis* the country in which it is providing services is not the factor which triggers the application of Community law. It is the fact that the company is established in a country other than that in which its potential customers are to be found. Thus the right to provide services has actually been invoked by nationals against their own state, when they have taken up residence abroad. Secondly, companies established in one member state and providing services in another through intermediaries may actually enjoy a legal advantage over companies doing business in the latter state through agencies, branches or subsidiaries. The latter are, in principle, subject to all the rules and regulations of the host state. The former, however, may not be required to comply with all the requirements of local law where this would place unreasonable burdens on a company from another member state and where the public interest is adequately safeguarded in the member state of establishment. For example, as we explain in the Case Study on pp. 139–45, the European Court has condemned rules imposed by a number of member states which required insurance undertakings to do business in those states through persons established in those states. In another series of cases the Court has condemned national laws which require undertakings which are licensed to carry out particular activities in one member state having to obtain a second licence to provide the same services in another member state where the licensing requirements in the first member state adequately safeguard all necessary requirements for the protection of the public interest.

Licences

While the right to set up any agency, branch or subsidiary in another member state is invaluable when commercial considerations merit it, the obligation to set up such a local establishment may be a high price to pay for what is still only the occasional prospect of business. National rules requiring such an establishment may well constitute improper restrictions on the freedom to provide services. This was the European Court's view of the requirement of the West German Insurance Supervision Law to the effect that foreign insurance undertakings must set up an establishment in West Germany and 'keep available there all the commercial documents relating to that establishment', for which separate accounts must be kept. In 1986 the European Court held that this requirement was incompatible with the right to provide services across national frontiers. The requirement of establishment imposed by the West German rule could only have been justified by the need to protect policy-holders. In the view of the European Court other means falling short of requiring a place of business on West German territory could have done this equally well. The legal proceedings referred to above were conducted by the Commission against four member states – Denmark, the Republic of Ireland, France and West Germany – in respect of these countries' national rules regulating the selling of insurance by foreign companies. These proceedings, and the Community rules on which they were based, provide an interesting illustration of the law relating to the provision of services (see pp. 139–45).

Insurance

The reason why companies established in one member state are entitled to do business in another without setting up a permanent place of business there is that such a requirement might unreasonably inflate their costs. The right to provide services caters for the firm seeking to enter a new market, or dealing only occasionally across a national frontier. National rules in the member states where services are provided can only be applied to the extent that the public interest requires it, and after due account is taken of the national rules applied to the company in the member state of establishment. In the case brought against West Germany concerning the West German Insurance Supervision Law referred to above, the European Court indicated that there were cases where a provider of services might be exempted altogether from the supervisory requirements of national law, where the services were being provided to commercial enterprises who could look after themselves and did not need the same degree of protection as consumers. It must be emphasised that this legal position, whereby the company is exempted from certain rules of the host state, can only arise in a case in which *services* are provided without a place of business being established in the host state. However, where a company *establishes* itself in another member state all the rules of that member state which apply to its own nationals apply equally to that company.

Harmonisation or mutual recognition and home country control

The removal of restrictions and the removal of discrimination to provide equal access does not itself create a single market. The existence of different laws, regulations and administrative requirements in the field of establishment and services has the practical effect that the Community market remains partitioned and compartmentalised. In order to create a single internal market, it is necessary to harmonise all domestic laws, to have a common regime throughout the Community or for member states to recognise each other's requirements as legally equivalent.

Reference has already been made to the opportunities now available to companies to establish agencies, branches or subsidiaries in other member states, and to conduct business activities in other member states through intermediaries without establishing a local presence. In order to facilitate such cross-border activity, EC rules have in important respects harmonised the national systems of company law and business regulation, thereby providing the underlying framework upon which implementing national rules are based.

When it comes to such matters as the protection of creditors and third parties dealing with a company, the obvious way forward is for the Community to lay down in its Directives detailed rules which are to be given similar effect under national law in all member states. This approach has much to be said for it, and certainly makes for equal

Equivalence

treatment for shareholders, creditors and third parties, and equal terms in these respects for establishment in each member state. It is however an approach which has its limitations. It is based on the assumption that commercial confidence in inter-state transactions will only flourish when the framework of company law and business regulation applicable in each member state is the same. Yet the Treaty of Rome itself describes one of the major aims of company law harmonisation as being to make safeguards for shareholders and third parties *'equivalent* throughout the Community' (Article 54(3)(g)).

Equivalent (rather than identical) standards in the member states have certainly provided the basis for facilitating cross-border trans-actions in other areas of Community law. For example, goods lawfully produced in one member state need not necessarily comply with all the technical standards applied in the various member states into which they are imported (such as the West German prohibition on the sale of beer containing even harmless artificial additives). Such goods can only be excluded by the state of proposed importation if they pose a sufficiently serious threat to public health or some other legitimate national interest compatible with the needs of the single market. Again, in the field of professional qualifications, including medical qualifications, there has been recognition of the equivalence of at least some of the various national degrees and diplomas, provided that they fulfil certain minimum standards laid down by Community law.

Techniques of harmonisation – from uniformity to equivalence

To reduce the complexities and costs of complying with a number of different requirements in different member states, the Community may co-ordinate, approximate or harmonise the relevant rules of national law, that is to say, lay down rules which must be adopted by all the member states. These rules may provide that certain business activities are always regulated in a certain way, irrespective of where they take place. For example, a condition of official listing on the stock exchange of any member state is that disclosure is made of certain matters required by Community law (see pp. 36–7). Compliance with these rules will be enforced by the appropriate authorities in each member state. It has already been pointed out that requiring the fulfilment of identical requirements in all member states may be unnecessary, and that recognition of equivalent standards may be a better approach, in particular to the question of harmonising the rules on the conduct of various types of business activities in the member states. In line with this approach, Community law may subject some matters to national supervision, subject to minimum Community requirements, and other matters to national law. Thus where companies with a head office in one member state have agencies or branches in a number of other member states, Community law may lay down certain requirements, for example, licensing, principally to the supervision of the member state where the head office is located, in liaison with the member states where the agencies and branches are actually located. Furthermore, the authorities of the member states where the agencies and branches are located may be permitted under Community law to apply and enforce their own rules to certain aspects of the conduct of business by those agencies and branches. This sort of division of responsibility is provided for in the insurance sector.

Financial services

This approach may well bear fruit if applied to the future harmonisation of company law strictly so-called, and indeed to the harmonisation of national rules on the conduct of particular classes of business activity. Directives in the field of banking and insurance already bear witness to the potential for such a flexible approach to harmonisation. In such fields a double need arises: to harmonise licensing requirements for companies intending to carry on the activities in question, and to lay down rules for the actual conduct of business by companies, or their agencies, branches and subsidiaries, in each member state. The Community is avoiding the approach of harmonising all aspects of licensing and regulation of the conduct of business, and is instead willing to divide responsibility between the authorities of the member state where the head office of a company is located, and the member state where the company or its agencies, branches or subsidiaries conduct business. The former authorities may (as in the case of insurance) be charged with enforcing rules subject to Community minimum standards, while the latter may be free to apply national rules to those matters allocated to them under Community Directives. The special responsibility vested in the member state of the head office for verifying compliance with Community minimum requirements is known as 'home country control' and will be of increasing practical importance for UK businesses which venture abroad while remaining subject to such home country control. As noted above, the supervision exercised by the member state in which the head office is located is not exclusive, and will be shared with the authorities in the member states where business is conducted. Close co-operation between the authorities in the various member states will be essential for the successful implementation of this imaginative and pragmatic form of harmonisation.

Home or host country control

The right of establishment granted by Community law includes a right for a company incorporated in one member state (the home member state) to establish a branch in another member state (the host member state). There is, however, a very important subsidiary question which is still a matter of controversy. This is the question of whose rules regulate the carrying on of its business in the host member state. The right of establishment also gives companies incorporated in one member state the right to establish agencies or subsidiaries in other member states. In addition, the Treaty of Rome also grants such companies the right to provide services from their home member state to residents of other member states. Similar problems may arise in these cases as well, even though not all the present Draft Directives themselves provide for these rights.

As a result of the right of establishment, a member state cannot keep out companies incorporated in other member states. Clearly, however, even if a company can freely establish a branch in a host member state it is also necessary to decide whether the conduct of that branch's business should be regulated by the home member state or the host member state. The question therefore arises as to whose rules should govern the conduct of the branch's business and this has given rise to much debate. The controversy can be summarised as the question of whether a branch of a company incorporated in one member state is to carry on business in its host member state under home country or host country control.

Manufacturing

Where the branch manufactures a product (such as a car) the standards it must comply with are those of the host member state; conversely, where it sells a product made in its home member state the manufacturing standards of the home member state are normally the relevant ones, although the rules of the host member state would apply to its advertising in that state provided that they can be justified as being for the public good. However, the provision of services by a branch does not clearly fall within either of these principles, because the services are provided from the host member state itself, and accordingly either alternative seems available. The problem is most crucial in the case of the provision of financial services such as banking or securities trading; the EC seems to prefer home country control but from the point of view of the investor in the host member state this is not necessarily the best solution, at least if the home member state's rules are more relaxed than those of the host member state.

Services

Indeed, the fundamental reason for the controversy is that the Draft Directives do not actually impose identical conduct of business rules. If they did, the only question would be the choice of regulatory authority and clearly each member state would want its own regulatory authority to supervise its nationals, even in the case of overseas branches. It is, however, interesting to note that at present the regulatory authorities under the Financial Services Act do not want to exercise jurisdiction over overseas branches of UK firms in normal circumstances. However, the position is not so straightforward in the absence of uniform standards. Even if the EC lays down minimum standards, each member state may be allowed by the relevant Directive to impose extra restrictions or requirements on its own nationals and, provided that they are not discriminatory, also on nationals of other member states. If, however, home country control is adopted, branches of companies incorporated in other member states will not be subject to the 'extra' restrictions or requirements imposed by the host member state, but will have to comply only with those imposed by their home member state. The present drafts of the Second Banking Directive and the Investment Services Directive do not in fact impose any minimum standards at all and, accordingly, the fundamental question is even more straightforward: whose national conduct of business rules apply? The EC may in due course agree a Conduct of Business Directive which will introduce some uniform or minimum EC rules, but at present we are talking about purely national legislation, albeit within the parameters allowed by the Treaty of Rome.

Investment services   The controversy is most acute in the case of the proposed Investment Services Directive, which, as its name implies, will grant a right of establishment to EC firms providing investment services (brokers and investment managers, for example). If a UK broker establishes a branch in France, the broker may without thinking about it prefer that that branch is subject to UK conduct of business rules rather than French because of course UK laws will be more familiar. However, if UK rules are more stringent or more restrictive than French rules, the branch would be at an immediate competitive disadvantage against its local competition. Conversely, if a French broker was to set up a branch in London and was subject to those more relaxed French rules, the branch would equally be at a competitive advantage as against UK firms. Accordingly, and since it seems to be accepted that the rules imposed under the Financial Services Act are more stringent than those on the Continent, it is in the interests of UK firms that host country control is adopted.

Indeed, it is only possible for there to be, as intended, a level playing-field for the provision of investment and banking services in any jurisdiction if all firms providing those services in that jurisdiction (whether local firms or branches of firms incorporated in other member states) are subject to the same rules. The level playing-field concept does not mean that a firm should be subject to the same rules throughout the EC, but that wherever it carries on business it is subject to the same rules as its local competitors.

The position may, however, be different where a firm merely

provides services in a particular member state without establishing a branch there; it has not chosen to establish itself in the host member state and there therefore does seem reasonable justification for home country rather than host country control of its activities. The latest draft of the Investment Services Directive is silent on responsibility for conduct of business rules (although this had been referred to in earlier drafts); as a result, member states seem to be free to impose their normal rules on branches established in their jurisdiction so far as that is permitted under the Treaty of Rome, and therefore host country control would apply. Conversely, the Second Banking Directive (which gives a right of establishment to EC 'credit institutions') seems to provide for home country control of banking services provided by branches. It is at present unclear on which side of the line investment services provided by credit institutions will fall. Even if home country control is adopted, however, certain matters may remain the responsibility of the host member state; for example, the Draft Second Banking Directive reserves monetary measures to the host member state and gives it principal responsibility for liquidity, and, in the field of insurance, technical reserves are also a matter for the host member state. The controversy will disappear once all the member states introduce equivalent conduct of business rules but that is unlikely to be achieved in the short or perhaps even in the medium term.

Authorisation
The controversy about which conduct of business rules apply to a branch is quite separate from the question of whether a firm needs to be authorised, or licensed, by the host member state in order to be able to establish a branch. The requirement for authorisation represents a barrier which can keep out foreign firms. Accordingly, the proposed Second Banking and Investment Services Directives prohibit member states from subjecting firms from other member states which wish to set up branches in their jurisdiction to their own authorisation requirements in the case of activities for which they are already authorised by their home member state. The question of authorisation and its concomitant question of adequate financial resources is therefore properly a subject for home country control and supervision. This, indeed, seems to be accepted at present, except in the case of insurance, where host member state authorisation is required. However, for home member state authorisation to work, member states clearly have to have confidence that all member states impose satisfactory conditions for authorisation. The approach taken by the EC is to impose not uniform standards but minimum standards. A company cannot be authorised if it does not comply with these minimum standards but each member state can impose additional standards of its own on its own nationals (in the case of financial resources requirements, for example). If they do so, however, this would put their own

nationals at a competitive disadvantage. None the less, it is fair to say that this concept of home country authorisation or the 'single passport' (as it has become known) provides a potent tool for the establishment of a single market in financial services.

The role of company law, business regulation and competition policy

Within this general framework of Community legislative action to establish a single market, EC company and competition laws are of pivotal importance for UK businesses. In the chapters that follow we explain these rules in detail; here we outline how Community rules on company law, business regulation and competition law integrate into the general structure for the creation of a single market described in this chapter.

Company law and business regulation

For companies established or providing services in different member states to have to adjust to different regulatory regimes may lead to a duplication of accounting, licensing and countless other requirements. This may act as a disincentive to penetrating other national markets. It may reduce the opportunities for benefiting from economies of scale. It is for these reasons that the Treaty of Rome provides:

- For co-ordinating the legal safeguards available for the protection of shareholders and others, with a view to making such safeguards equivalent throughout the Community (Article 54(3)(g))

- For co-ordinating the laws of the member states regulating the conduct of business activities in the member states (Article 57(2))

- For approximating those laws of the member states which directly affect the establishment or functioning of the Common Market (Article 100)

In Chapter 3 we examine how the Treaty rules are being implemented at Community level. Company law is examined against the wider background of the Community rules which grant equal access to the markets of other member states, and which harmonise the conditions for the exercise of particular types of business activity. Within the context of the creation of a single market in establishment and services described above, the Community rules seek to define conditions for equal access and to lay down uniform EC standards.

Equal access   The primary objective of the EC rules with which we are here concerned is to allow companies situated in one member state to provide services across national boundaries, or, if they wish, to set up agencies, branches or subsidiaries in other member states. It is easy to illustrate the rules of operation with an actual example. Not long ago, a Dutch business decided it would like to acquire the prestige of a UK PLC designation. A UK company was incorporated, which then became the holding company of a company set up to run the Dutch business. Unfortunately Dutch law did not provide equality of treatment in every respect for the subsidiaries of foreign parent companies – certain social security rules were not applicable to them. On a reference from a Dutch court, the European Court in Luxembourg held that the Dutch company was entitled to the same treatment as other Dutch companies, notwithstanding that it was the subsidiary of a UK parent. Whenever a company in one member state seeks to do business in another, whether by establishing a physical presence in the second state or not, Community law defines the conditions for equal access to the market of that state.

Common safeguards   If companies in Europe are to deal across national boundaries, it is important that investors, customers and creditors are able to deal with confidence with enterprises from other member states, whether directly, or through their subsidiaries and agencies. The Community has adopted two distinct approaches to maintaining public confidence in cross-border transactions:

National companies   • To date, in certain areas of company law, minimum standards have been laid down at Community level, and apply to companies throughout the EC, irrespective of where they are incorporated or have their central administration. Investors, customers and creditors can thus rest assured that these rules apply whatever the location of the business transaction in question, provided only that the companies concerned are incorporated in the EC. These minimum standards now comprise a significant part of the law applying to companies in the member states, and deal with such matters as the obligations of promoters, liabilities of companies, capitalisation, and the presentation of corporate accounts. Steps to provide common rules for employee participation in the management of public companies have been more controversial, and it has been strongly argued in the UK that a voluntary approach, reflecting the differing traditions of the member states in questions of employer–employee relations, is to be preferred to compulsory representation of employees on company boards.

EC corporate structures

- An alternative method of maintaining business confidence in cross-border transactions is to provide for the establishment of EC companies, which would be formed and wound up according to Community rules rather than the rules of any particular member state. Although this approach has not yet been formalised in the enactment of the proposed European Company Statute, this concept of a European company structure remains under consideration. Once again, the question of the role of employees in the proposed corporate structure has given rise to some disagreement in the Council. An important first step towards a truly European corporate entity has been taken with the issue of EC rules providing for the formation of a European Economic Interest Grouping (see Chapter 3). While the EC competition rules prohibit inter-company co-operation which stifles competition and innovation, recognition is given to the advantages which result from co-operation and joint ventures which have the overall effect of increasing competition in the Community and benefiting consumers. Such co-operation is particularly favoured when the participants are small and medium-sized undertakings.

Competition law

EC competition laws have a pre-eminent role in the development and creation of a single market. There is no better description of their importance in the matrix of the single market than in the extracts following. In the Commission's 17th Report on Competition Policy, 1988, the role of competition law is described thus:

As the completion of the internal market by 1992 gathers pace, competition policy is coming more to the fore. This fact is widely reflected in the economic and industrial policies of the member states and in the emphasis on competition policy even in member states which hitherto did not have a well-developed legislative and policy framework in the field of competition. There is an increasing awareness amongst the general public that the absence of an effective competition policy entails substantial costs since it is always the taxpayer who pays for unjustified state subsidies and the consumer who pays through higher prices and lower efficiency due to cartels, price fixing, abuses by dominant firms and other restrictive practices.

Such a description is complemented by Paolo Cecchini in his seminal study on the impact of 1992, *The European Challenge 1992* (Wildwood House, 1988), where he observes in relation to competition policy:

> Costs will come down, prices will follow as business, under the pressure of new rivals on previously protected markets, is forced to develop fresh responses to a novel and permanently changing situation. Ever-present competition will ensure the completion of a self-sustaining circle. The downward pressure on prices will in turn stimulate demand, giving companies the opportunity to increase output, to exploit resources better and to scale them up for European, and global competition.

The EC rules are designed to prevent business distortions of competition in the Common Market through cartels and abuses of dominant market positions. Companies intent on exploiting Europe's single market may well wish to enter into co-operative relationships and joint ventures with other companies. Yet when companies are contemplating co-operation with competitors or potential competitors it is important that they take advice on the application of the Community competition rules. Although restrictive agreements which affect inter-state trade are prohibited, the Community competition rules recognise the beneficial effects which certain agreements – albeit containing restrictive elements – have on the competitive climate in general and on the penetration of new markets in particular. In this sense the competition rules aim to promote competition by positive action. Agreements between even small and medium-sized companies doing business within the same member state may fall within the scope of the EC rules on restrictive trading agreements. Even those people unfamiliar with legal technicality may have encountered Article 85 of the Treaty of Rome, the Community's strict anti-cartel provision which aims to prevent agreements between businesses, which distort competition in the Common Market. It would be a futile exercise to dismantle the governmental walls which divide Europe only to have businesses painstakingly rebuild them. Yet the EC rules recognise – and this is of fundamental importance – that not all co-operation between companies, even competing companies, is likely to reduce the overall level of competition in the Common Market. Sometimes minor restrictions on competition imposed by agreement may lead to major increases in the ability of participating undertakings to compete in a larger market, and in such cases the EC competition rules give full recognition to the economic reality by allowing the Commission to grant exemption for agreements which contain restrictive clauses but

Article 85

Exemptions

nevertheless promote the production or distribution of goods or services and provide a fair share of the resulting benefit to consumers.

Article 86

Article 86 establishes a regime to prevent undertakings which enjoy a dominant market position in part of the Common Market from abusing that dominance so as to restrict competition and affect inter-state trade.

For these reasons the competition rules must be consulted if companies are planning distribution arrangements (for example, exclusive or selective distributorships) which inhibit the capacity of either party, or of third parties, to compete in the market.

In Part II detailed attention is paid both to securing compliance with the competition rules and seeking the protection of the competition rules against companies whose unfair practices threaten to unfairly damage the businesses of competitors.

Since many British companies seek growth in the single market through distribution, franchising or licensing arrangements in other member states, joint ventures involving R&D and specialisation, and takeovers and mergers, detailed consideration is given to these matters in Chapters 6, 7, 8 and 9. Reference is also made in Chapter 4 to the application of the Community rules limiting state subsidies to industry, since investment decisions may be influenced by the promise of tax advantages or other state aids. The emphasis throughout is on getting business done in the new commercial and legal environment. For the purpose of the EC rules in question is not to stultify business activity by excessive regulation; it is to facilitate commercial activities by recognising existing rules as equivalent, or, if necessary and appropriate, laying down uniform rules in all the member states. That too is the practical reality. In legal terms, Europe is increasingly 'open for business'.

3. Company law harmonisation and other developments

In the following sections, key harmonisation measures affecting company law in the Community are discussed, including the Proposed Fifth Directive on the structure of public companies, the proposed 'Vredeling Directive' on employee information and consultation, the Proposed Directives on insider dealing and the conduct of takeovers, Directives relating to branches and subsidiaries, the European Economic Interest Grouping and the proposals for a European Company.

A full table of company law harmonisation measures is set out on pp. 192–4.

Board structures and employee representation

At present in the UK, each company has a board of directors which manages its affairs; directors are elected, and may be removed, by shareholders in general meeting, and a general meeting normally also has a residual power, by a special resolution (proposed as such and carried by a 75 per cent majority of the shares voted), to give a management direction to the board. Employees have no statutory rights of management or even (with limited statutory exceptions) consultation, although the board must have regard to their interests and, in the case of a takeover, an offeror must state the consequences for employees.

Radical changes to this pattern are contained in the Proposal for a Fifth Company Law Directive, in terms of both board structure and employee participation. However, this Proposal was originally issued in 1972, and was re-issued in 1983 following discussions with the European Parliament and the Economic and Social Committee; its lack of progress reflects its controversial nature, and its future advance is unlikely to be rapid. However, it is possible that it will be adopted by a qualified majority voting procedure.

As regards board structure, the Proposal suggests that, for all public companies (PLCs), whether or not their shares are listed or otherwise publicly traded, a distinction should be drawn between directors responsible for 'supervision' on the one hand and 'management' on the other. This could be achieved in one of two defined ways: a two-tier board consisting of separate managing and supervisory boards (on the present West German model), or a one-tier board (as at present in the UK) but with a split of the management and supervisory functions.

If the two-tier board structure were used, then the management board would have the sole power of day-to-day management. Its members would be appointed by the supervisory board, who would have to be regularly informed as to the state of the company's affairs. The supervisory board would have a 'watchdog' role, with power to convene a general meeting if it thought it appropriate; in addition, a company's articles could provide that certain major actions of the management board required the supervisory board's consent.

If the one-tier board structure were used, then the executive directors would 'manage' and the non-executive directors would 'supervise'; to some extent, the boards of UK-listed companies are already moving towards this division, with the establishment of audit committees of non-executive directors to whom the auditors report any matter of concern in the company's draft accounts, and with the determination of the remuneration of executive directors by a committee of non-executive directors, who also deal with ethical matters and conflicts of interest.

The Proposal goes on to require that a public company with 1,000 or more employees (including employees of subsidiaries) within the Community must install a system of employee participation. The precise system will depend upon whether the company operates a two-tier or one-tier board structure, but in essence there are three options:

- Board representation for employees by way of electing between (at the option of the company) one-third and one-half of the supervisory directors or, alternatively, co-optation by the supervisory board subject to control by the general meeting or employees' representatives

- A works council (a body representative of all employees entitled to regular information and consultation)

- A collective agreement (i.e. with one or more trades unions) effectively giving the same rights as in one or other of the previous two options to the members of those trades unions (but not, it would seem, to all employees)

In the case of a two-tier board structure, the Proposal allows for the supervisory directors to be appointed by the supervisory board itself rather than shareholders or employees; in this case, employees would have a right of veto, as would shareholders.

The present UK government and the CBI have indicated strong opposition to these proposals, on the grounds that employee involvement is best left to a voluntary approach.

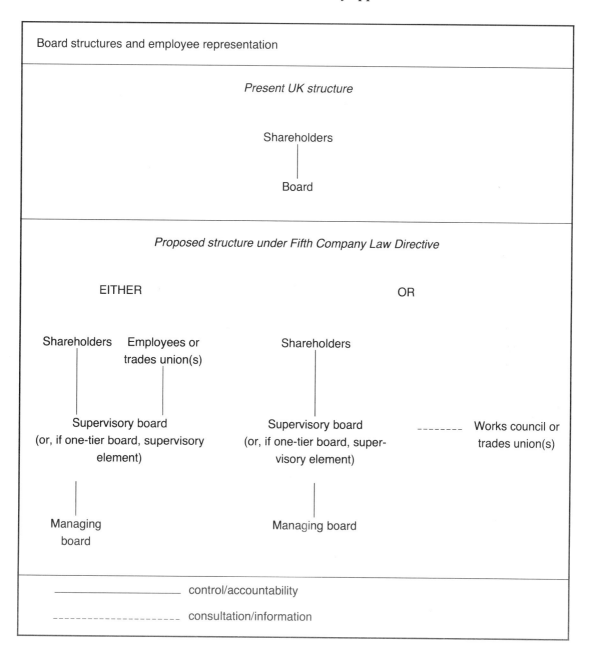

Board structures and employee representation

Present UK structure

Shareholders
|
Board

Proposed structure under Fifth Company Law Directive

EITHER   OR

Shareholders   Employees or   Shareholders
               trades union(s)

Supervisory board   Supervisory board ―――― Works council or
(or, if one-tier board, supervisory   (or, if one-tier board, super-   trades union(s)
element)   visory element)

Managing   Managing board
board

―――――――― control/accountability

------------- consultation/information

One particular matter of concern would be the election of directors by particular constituencies (shareholders on the one hand and employees on the other); if it were intended that they should represent those constituencies, this would conflict with the general principle of company law that *all* directors should look to the interests of the company as a whole. A possible solution to this particular problem would be a quotient system of election, under which shareholders and employees jointly elected the board, with their respective votes weighted to give employees between one-third and one-half of the value of the total votes cast.

These proposals interact with those for employee information (see p. 36) and for a European company (see pp. 46–8).

Accountancy and audits

A number of specific measures have been adopted or are in the pipeline in relation to accountancy and audit matters.

Company accounts

The Fourth Company Law Directive, to which UK legislative effect has already been given, regulated the form and content of company accounts; it is reflected in the accounting provisions of the 1985 Companies Act.

The Seventh Company Law Directive, dealing with consolidated accounts, and the Eighth Directive, on the qualification of auditors, are being implemented in the UK by the (1989) Companies Bill. They are relatively uncontroversial.

There is also a proposal to extend the Fourth Directive to both partnerships (whether limited or unlimited) and unlimited companies, in either case where the partners or shareholders themselves have limited liability. Under current proposals this will mean that a partnership or unlimited company so composed will be under the same accounting (and presumably also disclosure) requirements as a limited company. However, in appropriate cases, this disclosure requirement may be avoided by the use of an EEIG.

A Directive on the accounts of banks was adopted in December 1986, which has to be implemented by domestic legislation by the end of 1990. This effectively applies the Fourth and Seventh Company Law Directives to banks and other credit and financial institutions, which were originally excluded because it was believed that a separate directive would be necessary. In 1987, the Commission published a Proposal for a parallel Directive in relation to the accounts of insurance undertakings.

Auditing

For the longer term, it is worth noting that a number of the member states have a more independent system of audit, under which a company's accounts are audited, not by its own accountants, but by auditors who primarily owe a public interest duty. This may be a future subject for harmonisation, and indeed has been specifically reserved for further consideration by the Commission.

Branches and subsidiaries

One of the most interesting areas for future harmonisation relates to groups of companies, and branches of companies.

Under present UK law, a company has a separate legal personality; and its members, even if it is wholly owned by another company, are not – at any rate in theory – liable for its debts and other obligations. In practice, however, the dividing line has been somewhat blurred; the owners of a smaller company often give personal guarantees to its

Comfort letters

bankers, and a parent company will give, if not a formal guarantee, then a 'comfort letter' relating to its subsidiary's indebtedness to banks and others.

The dividing line became even more blurred in December 1987, when the Commercial Division of the High Court, in the landmark case of *Kleinwort Benson Limited v. Malaysian Mining Corporation Berhad*, effectively held that a comfort letter which does not expressly and precisely state that it has no contractual force will have such force, if its terms are sufficiently precise to be capable of interpretation. This came as no surprise to lawyers, who had long warned that the term 'comfort letter' was a misnomer, with each document having to be construed in accordance with its precise terms, but was a considerable shock to the business community. The decision was reversed on appeal on the facts. In any event, it is still the wiser course for a comfort letter expressly to exclude legal liability if such is the intention.

In the pipeline is a Draft Ninth Company Law Directive, which has not yet reached the stage of a formal proposal and indeed has not progressed since 1985. In effect, it seeks to establish a formal group structure where an undertaking controls a public company (whether or not its shares are listed) even if that company is not its subsidiary; an undertaking can be a person, firm or company. The suggested Directive's objective is to protect minority shareholders against abuses of power by regulating the way in which the controlling undertaking exercises its dominant influence over the public company by interfering in its management.

Where a dominant influence exists over a public company, the dominant undertaking will be liable for any damage suffered by the public company and, more radically, for any debts incurred by the public company as a result of its acting at the direction of the dominant undertaking, although this will seemingly not be the case if the dominant undertaking's influence is in fact exercised in the best interests of the public company.

Control contract

A different form of control liability will, however, apply if the dominant undertaking – whether or not a shareholder – has formalised its relationship with the public company concerned by a control contract which provides for it to manage the company and in which it offers the minority shareholders a buy-out or, at the shareholders' option, to pay them an annual protected dividend. The control contract must be registered and shareholders have three months after registration to demand to be bought out.

A control contract is subject to shareholder approval by a majority vote (including any shares held by the dominant undertaking: but, in the case of a company whose shares are listed or publicly traded, the domestic regulatory authority may – as the Stock Exchange presently does – ban an interested shareholder from voting in this type of situation); such a contract may therefore allow predators who have obtained board control of a company to make that company effectively subservient to an external body without the formalities of a takeover.

A control contract may be terminated by agreement, by notice or, in extreme cases, on an application to the court. Once a control contract has been entered into, the dominant undertaking and the public company will in effect be treated as a single entity. The dominant undertaking will be able to give binding directions to the public company in the light of the group's overall interest rather than that of the public company alone (so over-riding the present UK approach of treating companies as separate entities even if they are in a group). Conversely, and as the price for treating the company as its own, the dominant undertaking will be liable for the obligations of the company if the company defaults and this seemingly will apply even to pre-existing obligations; however, the dominant undertaking will be able to apply for relief from liability if it did not itself cause the company's default. The suggested Directive will impose substantial disclosure requirements relating to the exercise of management power by the dominant undertaking, if the public company is its subsidiary.

In its present form, this possible Directive is not significant for the UK; very few public companies in the UK are managed by a dominant undertaking. It is, however, worth noting that the number of public companies, and their proportion of the total number of companies, is significantly higher in other member states, so that this may in time be of concern to a UK company with a subsidiary in another member state. In addition, although the suggested Directive is limited to *public* companies, the accompanying explanatory note shows that consideration is being given to extending its scope to private companies, so that it would effectively apply to private companies which are subsidiaries of a public company (the normal UK group structure). It must be likely that in due course a parent company in the UK will be legally responsible for the debts of at least its wholly owned subsidiaries unless, perhaps, it files some sort of public disclaimer.

Compulsory acquisition rights

The suggested Directive will also grant important compulsory acquisition rights to the dominant undertaking if it has acquired a 90 per cent holding, whether or not there is a control contract. The compulsory acquisition procedures used in the UK after a takeover will therefore become available throughout the EC, and this may promote cross-border mergers.

Also under consideration, and effectively interlinked with the parent–subsidiary relationship (although progress on it has been faster), is a proposed Eleventh Company Law Directive, which prohibits any requirement for separate accounts for branches of companies incorporated in other member states and substitutes provisions compelling disclosure, in the member state in which a branch operates, of the affairs of the company (or, where it is a subsidiary of the group to which it belongs). Similar disclosure requirements will apply to non-EC companies but in their case these are *minima* only and other accounts can also be required, seemingly even those relating to the branch.

Disclosure

From a UK standpoint, this may be helpful. Similar disclosure provisions already operate in the UK in relation to overseas companies which have a place of business here (although the requirement to file group accounts would be new), whereas in other member states additional information may currently be required relating to that branch (e.g. branch accounts which would effectively reveal dealings between the branch and the rest of the company). If the proposed Directive is adopted, this additional information can no longer be required and this removes potential competitive disadvantages to which UK companies may otherwise be subject and which may constitute barriers to the right of establishment.

The stated intention of the Eleventh Directive is to harmonise the laws relating to subsidiaries and branches. At the moment, the establishment of a branch tends to require less documentation, formality and cost, while a subsidiary has the advantage of being a separate legal personality, with the result that disclosure requirements may not apply to the parent, and the subsidiary's debts will not necessarily become obligations of its parent in the event of insolvency. However, if the Eleventh Directive is implemented, this non-disclosure advantage may disappear and, similarly, if the Ninth Directive is put in place, and in due course extends to all subsidiaries (whether public or private companies), then this non-recourse advantage will also disappear in the circumstances specified in the Ninth Directive.

Insider dealing

In May 1987 the Commission issued a Proposal for a Directive to make insider dealing unlawful throughout the Community; an amended Proposal was issued in October 1988. The related domestic legislation will have to be enacted before the end of 1990.

For the UK, there will be no significant effect provided that the categorisation of confidential information follows that under present UK law. UK company law already incorporates most of the requirements (although some alterations may be necessary), and indeed the Proposal is largely modelled on the Company Securities (Insider Dealing) Act 1985, as amended by the Financial Services Act 1986.

The proposed Directive applies to all transferable securities traded on a stock exchange in a member state but in the case of off-market dealings it will permit a member state to limit the application of its domestic legislation (as the UK does at present) to dealings with or through a professional intermediary such as a stockbroker. The proposed Directive applies not only to listed securities, but also to those quoted or dealt in with less formality (e.g. on the British Unlisted Securities Market and the French Deuxième Marché) and to traded options related to them; this will be so even if they are issued by non-EC companies. This is wider than the scope of present UK law. State securities (e.g. gilt-edged stock) and local authority investments are, however, excluded. As already in the UK, it will render unlawful (although not necessarily in terms of criminal law: the penalties may only be civil but must be sufficiently dissuasive) the misuse or improper disclosure of unpublished price-sensitive information, either by insiders or by those who obtain the information from them. Under English law 'obtain', in this context, can be passive following a recent House of Lords decision.

Regulatory authority   Each member state will be the regulatory authority in relation to dealings on its own stock exchange; in the case of an off-market transaction, the member state where the 'victim' of the transaction is resident will have jurisdiction.

To prevent insider dealing, companies whose securities are publicly traded will be obliged promptly to announce price-sensitive information; similar obligations are already in place in the UK by reason of the Rules of The Stock Exchange and the City Code on Takeovers and Mergers, and this will impose similar disclosure requirements on other EC companies.

Finally, the proposed Directive will contain provisions on co-operation between the competent authorities in the various member states, for the exchange of information in particular.

Free movement of capital

Article 67 of the Treaty of Rome provided for the abolition of restrictions on the movement of capital within the Community during the first twelve years of the Community's existence. However, after initial strides towards the achievement of this objective, progress faltered – and even reversed, as some member states in the 1970s took advantage of the safeguard provisions of the Treaty of Rome to introduce restrictions on capital transactions which had already, in principle, been liberated.

The explosive development in the 1980s of the international financial markets made complete liberalisation a necessity, and this was achieved, following the Single European Act, by a 1988 Directive (known as 'the Article 67 Directive'). The Article 67 Directive, which requires the abolition of any domestic restrictions on movements of capital between persons resident in member states, must be implemented before 1 July 1990; Spain, Portugal, the Republic of Ireland and Greece are given transitional relief until the end of 1992, and Belgium and Luxembourg may temporarily continue to operate their present dual exchange market.

Investment

The Directive is not significant in terms of inward investment into the UK (exchange control was suspended in 1979 and abolished in 1987, although the Directive will prevent its reintroduction in relation to other member states). But outward investment from the UK into other member states will be de-restricted in terms of the domestic legislation of those member states. The Directive permits temporary protective measures, but any such measures cannot continue without the approval of the Council or in any event for longer than six months.

European Monetary System

A more sensitive area is that of actual currencies. The UK remains outside the exchange rate mechanism of the European Monetary System – notwithstanding that it has abolished exchange controls and that, in practice, it seeks to maintain a degree of stability in relation to the other European currencies – although, by issuing Treasury Bills denominated in ecu, it has given impetus to the development of the ecu as an eventual common European currency.

A European study group reported in April 1989 on concrete steps towards economic and monetary union including eventually a European central bank and a common currency. The present UK government has indicated hostility to the proposals.

Employee information and consultation

Since 1980 a proposal has been under discussion for a Directive which could require companies to introduce procedures for informing and consulting employees; it became known as the 'Vredeling Directive'. Two principal (albeit contradictory) difficulties arose: the belief of the governments of some member states (including the UK) that any such procedure should be voluntary, and the fact that Vredeling was not limited to collective representation of employees through trade unions.

The 'information' part of Vredeling, which would apply to employers with 1,000 or more employees, would require that information relating to the business as a whole, and to the employees' own particular subsidiaries or establishments, be supplied annually to employees' representatives. Such information would include the economic and financial state of the business, its forecast development, the present and anticipated pattern of employment and its investment prospects.

Management would also be obliged to consult employees' representatives on matters likely to have serious consequences for their interests, with a view to attempting to reach agreement. In the 1983 draft, such matters include major closures and relocations; substantial reductions or alterations in the business; major organisational changes, including those arising from new technologies; joint ventures; and health and safety. There will be an exception on the grounds of commercial secrecy.

The Commission may be producing a revised proposal in the course of 1989. Meanwhile, UK law has moved some way towards this concept, with companies with 250 or more employees obliged to state in their directors' report what action has been taken during the year on employee consultation and participation.

Stock exchange listings

The 1979 Admissions Directive established minimum requirements in relation to the full listing (not merely quotation or market dealing) of securities on a stock exchange in a member state; the related UK domestic legislation was incorporated in the 1986 Financial Services Act. There is, as yet, no mutual recognition of listings on different stock exchanges, but merely a requirement for co-operation if applications are made to different stock exchanges roughly contemporaneously.

The Listing Particulars Directive of 1980 sought to harmonise disclosure requirements, with a view to eventual mutual recognition of listing particulars. The UK disclosure requirements are imposed by the Financial Services Act (which requires all material matters to be disclosed) although the details are set out in the 'Admission of Securities to Listing' issued by The Stock Exchange.

Under the Listing Particulars Directive, it is a condition of admission to listing that the issuer publishes listing particulars which contain, in as easily analysable and comprehensive a form as possible, the applicable items listed in the Directive. The listing particulars may not be published until they have been approved by a competent authority in the member state; the competent authority in the UK is The Stock Exchange. Member states may allow the competent authority to provide for partial or complete exemption from the obligation to publish listing particulars in particular circumstances.

The mutual recognition provisions apply where applications are made simultaneously or within a short interval of one another for admission of the same securities to official listing on stock exchanges in two or more member states. If the securities are to be listed in the member state where the issuer has its registered office, the listing particulars must be drawn up under the laws of, and approved by, the competent authority in that member state. If the issuer is not incorporated in any of the member states where the securities are to be listed, the issuer must decide which of those member states is to have responsibility for approving the listing particulars; it must then draw up the listing particulars in accordance with the laws of that member state. Under these provisions, stock exchanges in one member state will have to accept listing particulars approved by the responsible competent authority in another. The Financial Services Act will need to be amended to implement these provisions.

The Directive also provides for the EC to enter into bilateral agreements with non-member states for mutual recognition of listing particulars.

The Disclosure Directive

Transparency

In December 1988, the EC adopted a Directive which will require the acquisition or disposal of major holdings in listed companies to be publicly notified. The Disclosure Directive lays down minimum disclosure requirements throughout the EC and is aimed at improving the transparency of the securities markets. As an important by-product it will also make it difficult for prospective bidders to build up stakes in secret. At the time of writing, the final text of the Directive has not yet been published. However, it is unlikely that the final text of the Council Directive is significantly different from the Draft approved by the Council in August 1988, which is described below. The Directive is to be implemented by 1 January 1991.

The Disclosure Directive applies to holdings in a company which is incorporated in a member state and whose shares are officially listed on a stock exchange in that or any other member state (an 'EC listed company'). It provides that anyone who acquires a holding (or increases an existing holding) in an EC-listed company above a series of specified thresholds must notify the company accordingly. Disposals reducing holdings below any of those thresholds also have to be notified. The notification requirement will apply to any investor, even if the investor is not EC-resident. However, the Directive does not apply to holdings in open-ended investment companies or other collective investment undertakings; nor does it apply to holdings in companies incorporated outside the EC, although such companies which are listed on a stock exchange in a member state must make a public announcement of changes in major holdings of which they become aware (even though there is no actual notification requirement).

However, there is no provision in the Disclosure Directive for permitting companies who are concerned as to who may be holding their shares (for example, in the case of an anticipated takeover) to require holders of voting rights to disclose their interests; there is therefore no equivalent of a notice under Section 212 of the 1985 Companies Act, and this may prove a deficiency in the new system.

The Disclosure Directive applies to changes in voting rights rather than share capital and this means that the notification requirement is therefore not dependent on having a beneficial interest in the shares. Indeed, in many EC jurisdictions (for example, the Netherlands) there is no concept of trust or, therefore, of beneficial interests; a person's rights to shares held by another on their behalf rest only in contract and therefore a notification requirement based on beneficial ownership would not work. In addition, notifiable holdings may vary significantly from shareholdings if certain classes of shares carry no votes, or where a stock exchange allows listed shares to have weighted voting rights. Moreover, it is unclear from the latest draft of the Directive whether all classes of voting shares in a listed company are included or only listed shares. Importantly, the Directive applies to all voting shares, even if they are bearer; it may therefore become impossible to shelter a major holding behind the anonymity of bearer shares.

Notification thresholds

The notification requirement applies at certain threshold levels, namely 10 per cent, 20 per cent, one-third, 50 per cent and two-thirds, although member states are given the option to have different thresholds in certain cases (for example a 25 per cent threshold instead of the 20 per cent and one-third thresholds). This is a different approach to present UK practice, which requires notification of any percentage increase or decrease at levels at or above the single threshold level of 5 per cent (which will come down to 3 per cent under the 1989 Companies Bill). The Directive allows more stringent requirements and therefore it would seem that the present UK practice (and its lower initial threshold) can be continued, which may help UK companies fearful of predators. If it is required, the notification must be made within seven calendar days and must specify the proportion of voting rights actually held and, if required by the member state, the proportion of share capital. The notification must be made not only to the EC-listed company itself but also to the competent authority (in the case of the UK, probably the Stock Exchange). Under Stock Exchange rules, it is the company which is required to notify the Exchange and accordingly this will be an important change in practice. The EC-listed company must make a public announcement about the acquisition or disposal in all member states where its shares are listed within ten calendar days, although member states can require disclosure to be made by the competent authority rather than the EC-listed company itself. The information must be published in at least one newspaper circulating in the member state concerned, or must be made available in specified locations.

Voting rights

There are detailed provisions which, following the precedent set by the 1985 Companies Act in the same context, attribute voting rights held by one person to another. This would apply, for example, in the case of nominees and controlled companies and also (as in the case of the 1985 Companies Act) where there is a written agreement relating to the exercise of voting rights in concert; the test of control is, in general terms, a subsidiary test rather than the UK's present one-third voting-power test, which can therefore be continued. In addition, there are attributed to lenders voting rights on shares charged to them (except where they are controlled by the chargor). Finally, and significantly, voting rights exercisable by discretionary portfolio managers are attributed to them (although member states are allowed to postpone the notification requirement in this last case so that it is tied to general meetings). Where the notification is made by a parent company, however, its subsidiaries do not have to make their own

Exemptions

notification. In addition, member states are allowed to exempt from the notification requirement what are termed 'professional dealers in securities' if they do not use the securities acquired to interfere in the company's management; the expression 'professional dealers in securities' may be confined to market makers (as under the 1985 Companies Act) but the expression does seem wide enough to include own account dealers as well and this is supported by the fact that the exemption applies even to professional dealers who are not members of a stock exchange, provided that they are authorised or supervised by a competent authority (an investment bank, for example).

The Disclosure Directive also allows competent authorities to exempt EC-listed companies from the requirement to notify the public if the disclosure would be contrary to the public interest or seriously detrimental to the company concerned (provided that the public would not be misled); this does not, however, exempt a person acquiring voting rights from having to disclose them to the company if a relevant threshold is reached.

Finally, the Disclosure Directive contains a transitional provision which is intended to inform companies of the up-to-date position when the Directive is implemented. It provides that existing holdings of 10 per cent or more must be notified to the EC-listed company at the first annual general meeting which takes place more than three months after the Directive has been implemented; they must be notified to the competent authority at the same time and must be made public within one month after the meeting.

The Takeover Directive

In December 1988 the Commission adopted a Proposal for a Directive on takeovers. The proposed Directive aims to harmonise the laws of member states on the conduct of takeovers, mergers or exchanges of securities in the case of public companies (whether or not quoted but small unquoted companies are excluded). The aim is to require full disclosure, fairness and equal treatment of shareholders in takeovers.

The stated approach of the Commission takes into account the fact that, in general, takeovers can be considered as a positive phenomenon, which calls for the identification by market forces of the more competitive businesses, and a restructuring of Community businesses, which is vital to match international competition. The Commission, by establishing a regime which promotes transparency, also wants to ensure that takeovers which are purely speculative in financing terms must be disclosed as such.

The Commission's proposals have as their background the fact that, although some member states have specific rules in this area, others have no legislation because takeovers are almost unknown in their countries (as is the case in Denmark and Greece). Among the member states which have specific legislation, the kinds of rules vary. Spain, France and Portugal have rules with legal force.

Belgium and Luxembourg follow decisions issued by their competent authorities. Other member states (West Germany, Italy, the Netherlands, the UK and the Republic of Ireland) have a voluntary code of conduct; the UK code, while theoretically voluntary, is in practical terms binding in the UK, albeit less so in the Republic of Ireland (even though there is a unified Stock Exchange).

The essence of the proposed Directive is to set out rules with the two-fold aim of ensuring the equality of treatment of shareholders in the target company and also obtaining full disclosure. The principal proposed rules are the following:

- A bid must be announced as soon as it is decided on, copies of the offer document must be given in advance to the target company's directors and offer periods must normally be restricted to not more than ten weeks after the publication of the offer document.

- Mandatory bids are required if a minimum holding is reached, and partial bids above this threshold are therefore prohibited, subject to exemptions granted by the regulatory authority. Accordingly, a person who intends to acquire or take his holding of voting rights on listed securities to a specific percentage of the target company's voting rights (one-third at most, but perhaps with lower thresholds in other member states) is normally required to make an offer for all the shares; as under existing UK practice, the holdings of concert parties must be included.

- An offer document must be issued and must contain certain required disclosures (the names of concert parties, for example); details of the offeror's holdings in the target company and those of concert parties; the offeror's intentions as to the utilisation of the assets and the continuity of the activities of the target company and the continued employment of its employees. Topically, the offer document must contain a statement as to the offeror's ability to pay any proposed cash consideration and must also indicate the contemplated level of future indebtedness (especially in the case of leveraged buy-outs which are often effectively financed by the target company). The offer document (and other relevant documents) must be given by the target company to the trade union or other representatives of its employees.

- The offeror must use an authorised issuing house or broker or an authorised credit institution; this is a useful step towards enforcing compliance and follows existing UK practice.

- Following current UK rules, dealings by holders of 1 per cent or more of the voting rights must be disclosed.

The directors of the target company will have to give their opinion on the offer and make it clear whether or not they recommend it.

Defensive measures

The proposed Directive also provides for the circumstances in which defensive measures can be adopted after the announcement of an offer. In particular, the board of directors of the target company must not issue new shares or convertible securities in order to frustrate the offer, or engage in manoeuvres such as the sale of assets without shareholder consent or consent from the regulatory authority. The whole question of poison pills is to be reviewed by the Commission.

Enforcement

The enforcement of the regulations provided for in the proposed Directive will be the responsibility of the relevant regulatory authority, which must be created in the member states where such a body does not already exist. That authority will have the power either to forbid the launch of the offer, or to require the offeror to publish a corrected offer when the information furnished by the offeror is insufficient.

So far as the UK is concerned, the proposed Directive contains little that is new in substance and, indeed, it shows clear signs of actually being based on the City Code on Takeovers and Mergers, which is the present UK rulebook for takeovers. Its adoption and implementation throughout the Community would therefore go a long way towards levelling the takeover playing-field for UK investors looking at opportunities in other member states. However, implementation of the Proposal will require a fundamental change in the present voluntary system under which takeover bids for UK public companies are regulated by a voluntary body (the Panel on Takeovers and Mergers) under the City Code, which does not have the force of law. The Code will have to be given the force of law and in some respects detailed adjustments will be necessary to conform with the requirements of the Directive. A regulatory body will have to be empowered by law to administer the new rules; however, as the proposed Directive allows the regulatory authority to delegate its powers to a private body, there is no reason why the Panel in its present form should not be given the necessary authority, with the result that changes in day-to-day practice may prove to be minimal. The Panel may, nevertheless, have to be supervised by the regulatory authority (for example, the DTI) and this would be novel. However, the decisions of the Panel are already subject to judicial review; the Panel is therefore already some way from being totally self-regulatory even now. In the case of bids across national borders within the EC, the relevant regulator is that of the member state where the target has its registered office.

The proposed Directive will not apply to bids for non-EC

Reciprocity

companies. Similarly, the Commission does not incorporate in the proposed Directive reciprocity requirements (similar to those in the proposed Second Banking Directive) in relation to bids from offerors in non-EC countries, which it regards as too wide a topic for a Directive on takeovers, although it is reviewing the 'hidden' barriers to takeovers in other countries. Instead, until further co-ordination can take place, the right of a member state to forbid a takeover offer launched by an offeror which is a national of or a corporate body from a non-EC country will continue. This is so particularly when the nationals and corporate bodies of the member states do not benefit from reciprocity in relation to a takeover of a body corporate situated in these third countries. The Community intends to start discussions on reciprocity with other countries, especially in the OECD.

The European Economic Interest Grouping

In contrast to the grander scale of the European Company (see pp. 46–8), the European Economic Interest Grouping (EEIG) is a flexible vehicle permitting companies and others to co-operate within the Community on a cross-border basis. It was originally inspired by a French invention, the Groupement d'Intérêt Économique, allowing an association of companies wishing to pool resources such as staff or offices to pursue a particular activity without affecting their individual independence, or creating separate limited liability or a new profit centre.

Go to work on an EEIG

The essence of an EEIG is a joint venture vehicle which has the mixed characteristics of an unlimited company and a partnership. It cannot be an enterprise on its own, but enables its members to facilitate or develop their economic activities though a vehicle (which may have a legal personality), while the members remain jointly and severally liable for the debts of the combined enterprise and are taxed directly on their respective proportionate shares of the profits.

Formation

An EEIG may be formed by persons, firms or companies (or indeed other bodies, whether incorporated or not) in the EC, but not by non-EC bodies; individuals must be carrying on a trading or service activity (including the provision of professional services) and bodies may be public or quasi-public. As the intention is to promote cross-border co-operation, members of an EEIG must come from at least two member states. An EEIG may not have more than 500 employees, nor offer participations to the public.

The contract establishing an EEIG must be filed with the designated Registrar in the member state (or part thereof) where the EEIG has its official address; such registration confers full legal capacity on the EEIG throughout the Community. It is up to each member state to decide whether an EEIG registered by it should have separate legal personality. The UK has decided that UK-registered EEIGs should be treated as bodies corporate with separate legal personalities like companies and should be registered with the Registrar of Companies.

An EEIG may be registered after 30 June 1989; the Department of Trade and Industry has just issued the relevant regulations, as has the Treasury so far as tax transparency is concerned.

Constitution

The Regulation governing EEIGs is conceptually similar to the UK Partnership Act of 1890. A broad constitutional framework is created, with a limited number of mandatory requirements, some optional features and then a range of matters on which the framework operates unless the related contract specifically provides otherwise.

An EEIG has two mandatory constitutional organs: its members acting collectively, and one or more managers. Any additional constitutional organs are permitted.

The members have one vote each, unless the related contract provides otherwise (but no single member may have a majority of the votes). Unless the contract otherwise provides (which, in relation to some fundamental matters, it may not), unanimity is required on a number of defined key decisions, e.g. objects, voting rights or the extension of an original agreed life.

Although a member state may limit the number of members of an EEIG to twenty, it is envisaged that, in the UK, professional partnerships which may have over twenty members will be treated as a single member.

Management and financing

The manager(s) must be natural person(s), or, if so permitted in the member state of registration, a company which designates individuals whose details are then filed as if they were the managers and who then have similar obligations.

Any manager will (with certain limited exceptions) have power to bind the EEIG *vis-à-vis* third parties, unless the related contract provides that only two or more managers may so bind it and is gazetted accordingly.

An EEIG does not have to be formed with a capital, but may be financed in a number of ways (e.g. the provision of assets or services) or even not at all if participants consider that it can operate on the basis of current account facilities from any of the participants and/or a bank.

Using an EEIG

Although it is not possible to foresee exactly the principal uses to which EEIGs will be put, there are a number of significant pointers.

Flexibility   Firstly, the structure of the EEIG is flexible; accordingly, one participant could contribute capital (if indeed any is needed), another know-how and a third services. Cross-frontier research and development (including data processing), joint manufacturing or purchasing, marketing and professional services (particularly with a joint database) seem obvious candidates in this connection; distribution arrangements particularly, where the manufacturer provides the goods and the agent contributes the legwork, seem naturally suited to an EEIG.

Co-ordination   Secondly, the EEIG can be used either to co-ordinate the activities of its participants, or to extend their range. These two facets are complementary rather than necessarily exclusive – an EEIG could come together as a multi-disciplinary vehicle to tender for a construction, engineering or hi-tech project, whether within or outside the Community. If the tender was accepted, the various obligations could be divided amongst its members, while the EEIG itself became effectively the project manager, with a co-ordinating role. This could, for example, provide a convenient structure for multi-national aircraft or defence projects.

Cross-frontier property joint ventures might also be suited to an EEIG, particularly where the parties wish to signal that they have not formed a legal partnership through their joint activity.

Even though the whole range of potential uses of EEIGs may not yet be apparent, there can be no doubt but that any future joint ventures (whether or not traditionally structured as such), and indeed any existing ones, will be reconsidered in the light of this new corporate animal – a hybrid with infinite powers of reproduction. However, it **Competition rules** must not be forgotten that the EC competition rules on joint ventures will still apply. A joint venture between competitors or potential competitors may infringe Article 85 of the Treaty of Rome if the participants could reasonably have been expected to enter the market individually, and in such cases the creation of an EEIG will not obviate the need to seek an exemption, or at least a comfort letter, from the Commission. The Commission will need to be satisfied that the economic benefits to the market and the consumer will outweigh any anti-competitive effects. (See pp. 102–6.)

Many ventures which begin life as EEIGs will, if successful, need to progress to full integration, earning their own profits, enjoying limited liability and providing a basis on which capital can be raised from institutions or the public. The new European Company may well prove to be the Eurochicken into which EEIGs will hatch, if the Commission succeeds in its renewed efforts to overcome the various problems currently inhibiting its birth.

The European Company

The Commission hopes that by 1992 it will have established a new form of corporate vehicle – a European Company, or Societas Europaea (SE), incorporated in Europe (and registered with the Court in Luxembourg under a distinctive European Company Statute), albeit domiciled in a particular member state. An SE, which will be a company that has legal personality throughout the Community, could act either as a holding company for a plurality of subsidiaries in different member states, or itself be jointly owned by companies from different member states.

The intended role of the SE is to facilitate cross-border co-operation by means of large-scale mergers and associations (as opposed to smaller-scale ventures, for which the EEIG is designed).

The idea has been in the course of discussion since 1970; the delay has largely been caused by the related proposals on board structure and employee representation. In mid-1988 the Commission, in an effort to speed progress, addressed a formal Memorandum to the European Parliament inviting comments with a view to publishing a new Proposal at the beginning of 1989. The Commission's view is that increased cross-border co-operation in the form of mergers and associations is imperative for the benefit of the Community, in order to enable European business to compete more efficiently in world markets against US and Japanese megaliths, for example. In March 1989, the Parliament overwhelmingly supported the Proposal.

Key features

If the Commission's Memorandum is followed, the Statute will, on various routine matters, follow company law as harmonised by the various Directives referred to above. In particular, it would follow the Fifth Directive as regards employee representation. However, it would have two distinct features.

Mergers

Firstly, on the structural side, where an SE was superimposed on two or more other companies as a new holding company, there would be an easy mechanism for the resultant merger, with both original companies being automatically dissolved and their former share-holders automatically becoming members of the SE – rather like a UK Scheme of Arrangement approved by the High Court.

Tax benefits

Secondly, there would be two tax benefits. The profits and losses of a group headed by an SE would be fully offsettable, and dividends would attract a common tax treatment throughout the Community.

Problems of an SE

It has to be said, however, that the Proposal is subject to a number of criticisms. One is that the proposed tax treatment has not been agreed, and in some cases is being strongly resisted, at member state level. The other is that the element of employee representation is perceived by some – including the UK government and the CBI – as a way of pre-empting the present discussion on the proposed Fifth Directive.

Uses of an SE

It is difficult to give a confident forecast of the use that will be made of the SE.

Firstly, it is uncertain whether (and, if so, on what conditions) it will come into being: the long period of gestation and the outstanding issues on board structure and employee representation do not augur well for a speedy birth.

Secondly, its advantages in terms of mergers, while real in terms of merger procedure and taxation, are not so overwhelming as to guarantee its use (as opposed to, say, a company in a country such as Luxembourg, the Netherlands or a suitable tax haven), particularly if there are perceived concomitant disadvantages (in terms of board structure and employee representation, for example). Only if these disadvantages disappeared, and/or further relative advantages were put in place (e.g. by reason of adverse changes to the present mergers regime in terms of taxation or otherwise), would it be likely for the SE to become a creature of common use.

II
Competition

4. Living with the competition rules

The EC competition rules

The competition rules of the Treaty of Rome represent the most effective means available to businesses, both large and small alike, of ensuring that the Common Market operates effectively and fairly. In the 1985 White Paper 'Completing the internal market' this fundamental role for competition policy was recognised by the Commission, when it stated:

> As the Community moves to complete the internal market, it will be necessary to ensure that anti-competitive practices do not engender new forms of local protectionism which would only lead to re-partitioning of the market.

Articles 85 and 86 of the Treaty of Rome, the text of which is set out in Appendix 1, define the framework for the operation of the Community competition rules. Although both Treaty of Rome articles are expressed in terms of prohibition of certain forms of conduct, they can often be utilised by businesses as positive tools in the development of a Community business strategy.

Article 85

Article 85 prohibits:

- Agreements between undertakings
- Decisions by associations of undertakings or concerted practices (which we refer to in this book as 'arrangements')

Exemptions

which affect trade between member states and which prevent, restrict or distort competition within the Common Market. It recognises that competition is not an end in itself by providing a procedure whereby, although certain agreements or arrangements may prevent, restrict or distort competition, they may none the less improve the production or distribution of goods or promote technical or economic progress to the benefit of consumers. In those circumstances Article 85(3) provides for an exemption procedure.

Article 86

Article 86 prohibits the abuse of dominant market positions within

51

the Common Market in so far as it may affect trade between member states: the fact that a business has a dominant or monopoly position is not in itself prohibited.

Although Articles 85 and 86 describe a number of examples of anti-competitive behaviour, these are not exhaustive; any agreement, arrangement or conduct which actually or potentially affects trade in the Community and has an anti-competitive object or effect falls for consideration under Articles 85 and 86.

Impact on UK businesses

All businesses, whether trading as companies, partnerships, state corporations, agricultural co-operatives, trade associations or sole traders and whether for profit or not, must have regard to the competition rules of the Treaty of Rome. Agreements between trading parties made within a governmental framework fall within Article 85. For example, in a Commission decision in 1982 a network of price-fixing agreements within a trade association in the cognac industry established in France by statute was held to infringe Article 85, despite the fact that the association's board operated under government supervision.

Poacher or gamekeeper

The competition rules must be regarded as a double-edged sword by businesses. On the one hand the UK business entering EC markets is acting as a poacher in what has traditionally been regarded as territory belonging to other EC businesses. In those markets, EC competition rules can break down private barriers to trade. The barriers take on a variety of forms including cartel agreements or arrangements, national market organisations (such as co-operatives or trade associations) which discriminate against other EC nationals, and abusive monopolisation of markets. Conversely, the competition rules can be invoked by businesses as a 'sword' to cut away the private barriers to trade. Here, the same businesses must always remain vigilant that their arrangements, agreements and conduct conform with EC competition rules. Otherwise there is a risk of coming under attack for not complying with Community competition law requirements.

Whether the business is poacher or gamekeeper, the legal consequences of not complying with the Community competition rules are serious and include:

- Finding that any agreement or arrangement in conflict with Article 85 is void

- Fines of up to 1,000,000 ecu (£650,000) or 10 per cent of an undertaking's turnover, whichever is the greater (for these purposes, however, where an undertaking is part of a group, 'turnover' relates to the group's turnover)

- Civil proceedings before the domestic courts of any member state for an injunction and/or damages based on the competition rules of the Treaty of Rome

- Surveillance by the Commission of the operation of all future agreements or marketing policies

Scope of EC competition rules

Businesses should not be misled into thinking that, because Articles 85 and 86 are expressed to apply where there is an effect on inter-state trade, the agreement or abusive conduct has to be concluded within the EC to fall within their scope of application. The competition rules apply to all cases where the agreement, conduct or practices produce an effect on the normal patterns of trade or have a 'repercussion' on the competitive structure of a market thereby affecting trade between member states. Article 85 applies to undertakings established outside the EC if their agreement is implemented within the Community. Selling into the Community from abroad is itself sufficient to establish jurisdiction over anti-competitive behaviour by a supplier, although in a recent case the European Court held that a trade association which was established outside the Community and had no part in implementing a price agreement which infringed Article 85 is not subject to the EC competition rules. On occasions the effect on inter-state trade is tenuous, but none the less the competition rules have been applied.

Example

The European Court established in 1967 that a 'network' of agreements in a single member state, such as exclusive supply agreements of the type entered into by breweries and oil companies with their retail outlets, may collectively affect trade between member states for the purposes of Article 85 if market analysis shows that the overall effect of the agreements is to shut off a substantial proportion of the market in that state from other suppliers.

Example

The Commission has held that a non-competition clause in an agreement for the sale of a chemical marketing business between two nationals within the same member state none the less affected inter-state trade 'since it affects goods and services which . . . could be the subject of trade between member states'.

> **Example**
>
> The Court has held that the fact that a competitor's production is exported outside the single market does not prevent the possibility of the competitive structure within the relevant Community market being affected.

> **Example**
>
> The Court has held that, although an agreement concerned the actions of a trade association operating solely within one member state, since the subject matter of the agreement related to products traded between member states, Article 85 applied.

All business activities are encompassed by the competition rules. In this sense the reference to 'trade' in Articles 85 and 86 is misleading and all economic activities including the supply of goods or services (including financial services), broadcasting or communications generally, the exercise of intellectual property rights, or the carrying on of any other trade or profession are encompassed by the competition rules. On 22 December 1986 the Council of Ministers adopted four Regulations, the effect of which was to implement the application of the competition rules of the Treaty of Rome to the transport sector.

Public undertakings

Article 90

Telecommunications

Undertakings entrusted with the operation of 'services of general economic interest' or 'having the character of a revenue-producing monopoly' have a special status, and under certain circumstances defined in Article 90 of the Treaty of Rome those special activities may be exempt from the competition rules. Unless the Community has enacted legislation to apply the competition rules specifically to the activities of such undertakings, as it has recently done in the telecommunications sector, many public utilities such as water authorities, state postal services or state railways fall outside the competition rules. However, for this provision to apply, the special functions of the undertaking must have been conferred by virtue of an act of public authority. Therefore in one case the Commission refused to apply the provision to a Eurocheque clearing system which, although receiving the support of individual member states, was not established by legislation in those member states. In every case careful scrutiny of the precise structure of a public undertaking is necessary to ascertain whether it falls within the exemption.

Agricultural products

It should be remembered that agricultural products may require consideration of special competition rules (in particular, the rules on restrictive agreements and state subsidies may not automatically apply). Agricultural products for this purpose are only those listed in Annex II of the Treaty of Rome. Thus, fur skins are not to be regarded as agricultural products, since they do not appear in Annex II, and the normal competition rules apply (see the Hudson's Bay case study pp. 146–50). Special competition considerations arise if the products do appear in Annex II, whether they are subject to a common organisation of the market (which most products now are), or a national organisation of the market (which few products now are). Where products are still subject to a national organisation of the market, and the conditions under which the goods are marketed leads to distortion of the terms of competition under which similar goods are marketed in other member states, the Commission may impose compensatory charges upon exports of the product from the member state of origin. Ethyl alcohol of agricultural origin produced in France has given rise to such problems in the past, and complaints to the Commission have led to charges being imposed on several occasions, in order to protect alcohol producers in the other member states from unfair competition. France unsuccessfully challenged the Commission's authority to increase the charges before the European Court.

Dumping of products from outside the Community

GATT

It is not only anti-competitive practices within the Community which may threaten the legitimate business interests of companies trading in the single market. Dumping of products originating in countries outside the EC ('third countries'), that is to say disposing of products on the Community market at prices below the normal price on the home market, is internationally recognised as an unfair trading practice, and anti-dumping duties are permitted under the terms of the General Agreement on Tariffs and Trade if the dumping is causing injury. A Community Regulation provides for the imposition of such duties provisionally by the Commission for a limited period and then by the Council in the event that investigation by the Commission shows the dumped products of third-country origin are causing material injury to a Community industry. This form of protection for EC business is quite independent of the extent of their intra-Community trading activities.

The appropriate method of securing investigation and possible action is by making a complaint to the Commission. A reasoned case supported by evidence of both dumping and the injury it has caused is necessary and law firms specialising in Community law will be familiar with the appropriate procedures. Should the Commission reject a complaint made by a company alleging material injury to its commercial interests, and should the complainants be advised that the Commission has failed to make a proper appraisal of the situation, an appeal to the European Court may be made. In one case the Commission responded favourably to a complaint by imposing a provisional anti-dumping duty on certain imported watches which was in due course replaced by a definitive duty imposed by the Council. The complainant company was however of the opinion that the duty imposed was too low, and challenged the duty before the European Court on the ground that the Commission had not placed all relevant information at the disposal of the complainant, so as to allow the complainant to protect its interests, and that accordingly the duty was void. The Court upheld this argument, and ruled that the challenged duty should remain in force only until the Commission had taken steps to comply with the terms of the Court's judgment.

State aids

One way in which the terms of competition in the single market may be affected is by granting state subsidies which favour certain undertakings or the production of certain goods in such a way as to affect inter-state trade. The Treaty of Rome does not regard all state subsidies as incompatible with the Common Market; indeed, subsidies to consumers, and aid to seriously underdeveloped areas, are both regarded as being compatible with Community law.

Pre-notification

In order to secure compliance with the Treaty of Rome, the national authorities in the member states (including regional and local authorities) are bound to inform the Commission in advance of any plans to grant subsidies or to alter the terms of existing subsidies. This is to allow the Commission an opportunity to determine whether or not the aid in question is compatible with the Treaty of Rome. If an aid is granted in violation of the Community rules, the national authorities may be required by the Commission to recover the money from the beneficiary companies. It follows from this that some national legal environments are actually too good to last. Furthermore, it is open to a

Complaints

company to complain that a competitor has received a subsidiary from a public authority which is incompatible with the Treaty of Rome.

Proceedings may be instituted before a national court, and such proceedings have been successfully brought in the UK. A complaint may also be made to the Commission. As noted above, this may result in an order for recovery of the aid. Rejection of a complaint by the Commission may lead to proceedings before the European Court by the complainant, where the complainant alleges a direct and adverse effect on its market position as a result of the state subsidy of which complaint is made. In order to establish the legitimacy of its interest in such a case, a complainant would be well advised to participate fully in the Commission's investigation of its complaint, and produce evidence of injury to its business.

Defences to market dominance and anti-competitive behaviour

Not all agreements or arrangements which have a restrictive effect on competition are prohibited by EC competition rules. Equally, market dominance is not in itself unlawful under Article 86 of the Treaty of Rome. The Treaty provisions endeavour to establish a system of workable competition to maintain a choice for consumers, purchasers and suppliers, and to ensure that market entry remains unhindered by anti-competitive practices while at the same time supply and demand are allowed to operate freely, so ensuring that the prices at which goods are sold in the market place are competitive. In deciding a

Business strategy
strategy for the single market, UK businesses must plan and structure their policies to minimise their exposure and maximise the benefits they can draw from EC competition rules.

How to avoid Article 85

The Commission, which (pursuant to Article 87 of the Treaty of Rome and secondary Community legislation) is charged with the primary task of enforcing the competition rules, has defined a number of instances where restrictive agreements or arrangements fall outside the scope of application of Article 85.

First, there has to be an agreement between economically independent undertakings. Where one party has no commercial autonomy *vis-à-vis* another, it is treated as part of the same economic grouping and therefore not subject to Article 85, although if it is in a dominant position Article 86 may apply.

> **Example**
>
> Agreements between a parent company and its own subsidiary or between two companies which are under the common control of a third party are not caught by the competition rules because a subsidiary is not considered to have any economic freedom to determine its own course of action and therefore is treated as the same economic unit as its parent company.

> **Example**
>
> A commercial agent, having no commercial or economic entity as its principal.

> **Example**
>
> Agreements between a company and its employees are treated as falling outside Article 85 because the employee has no economic freedom.

Second, as noted above, there has to be an effect on inter-state trade. Where an agreement does not produce an appreciable effect on inter-state trade, Article 85 does not apply. Present guidelines are that, if goods or services covered by an agreement or arrangement or other goods and services perceived by consumers as equivalent do not **5 per cent limit** represent more than 5 per cent of the total market in an area of the EC affected by the agreement and the aggregate turnover of the participants in the respective group does not exceed 200 million ecu (£130 million), EC competition rules will not apply. Businesses should, however, be careful with these guidelines; they have no legal effect and the application of this *de minimis* rule, and market shares and turnover, can change during the currency of agreements.

Third, certain categories of restrictions on competition may not within their economic context be of such a nature to fall within Article 85. Even if Article 85 (1) applies to particular agreements or arrangements, if it can be shown that they benefit the production or distribution of goods or services so that the consumer benefits outweigh the restrictions on competition in the agreement, they may be exempt pursuant to Article 85(3). There are two types of Article 85(3) exemption.

Block exemptions The first type consist of block exemptions, in which the Commission defines the conditions where restrictions in certain categories of agreements are exempt. In addition to block exemptions which apply to the regulations implementing the competition rules to the air and

Black clauses

maritime sectors, block exemptions have been enacted to cover exclusive supply and distribution agreements, patent licensing agreements, know-how licensing agreements, franchising agreements, motor vehicle distribution and servicing agreements, specialisation agreements and research and development agreements. The structure of these exemptions is broadly the same. They define those clauses which can be included in agreements without losing the benefits of the exemption, and so-called 'black' clauses which if present in an agreement result in it losing the benefit of the exemption, and clauses which are not generally restrictive of competition and whose presence will not affect the exemption. The patent licensing, know-how, franchising, motor vehicle, and research and development block exemptions also provide a special 'opposition' procedure whereby if an agreement satisfying the basic requirements of the exemption, and not containing any black clauses, but containing other restrictions on competition which do not affect competition is notified to the Commission and not opposed by the Commission within six months of notification, exemption will automatically be conferred. As we explain further in Chapter 7 in relation to certain marketing arrangements, the careful planning and drafting of the various categories of agreement covered by block exemptions is of pivotal importance in commercial and corporate planning as a defence to those who may wish to attack commercial agreements of their competitors.

Individual exemption

Any agreement or arrangement which is not covered by a block exemption can benefit from an individual exemption by notification to the Commission. Only the Commission can grant an exemption, and notification generally provides immunity from fines although, in the case of a particularly clear infringement of the Treaty of Rome in notified agreements, the Commission can issue preliminary decisions removing the immunity from fines to prevent misuse of the notification procedure. Notification does not confer provisional validity. However, if an exemption is granted, it will generally render the agreement retroactively valid from the date of notification. Certain types of agreement will seldom if ever qualify for exemption, for example those which restrict competition so as to affect inter-state trade and contain export bans, maintain retail prices or lead to absolute territorial protection of national markets.

There are a number of circumstances in which the Commission may consider that a restriction on competition does not of itself fall within Article 85(1) because of the economic context in which it operates or alternatively where it is appropriate to grant individual exemptions. Examples of the granting of negative clearances or individual exemptions by the Commission and confirmed by the European Court in recent years include:

- Restrictions contained in franchise agreements where the Commission is satisfied that these are indispensable to the preservation of the identity and reputation of the franchise network

- Exclusive licence agreements (whether of patented goods, trademarks or other intellectual property interests) which allow new markets to be penetrated or new products to be licensed which may otherwise not be so exploited to be exploited or launched

- Restrictions by the vendor of a business not to compete with the purchaser provided that the restriction is reasonable in time and scope

- Joint ventures and restructuring agreements with capacity reduction for industries in crisis

Defences to monopolisation of markets

Market dominance is in itself not prohibited by the Treaty of Rome. However the case law of the European Court makes it clear that, irrespective of how undertakings become dominant, such undertakings have a special responsibility not to allow their conduct to impair genuine undistorted competition within the Common Market.

An undertaking may be in a dominant position if in the relevant product market it is in a position where, as a result of its economic strength, it is able to hinder effective competition by behaving to an appreciable extent independently of its competitors without taking into account customer and consumer demands.

In determining the existence of a dominant position, market shares are not in themselves determinant but the structure of competition may be.

Example

In a case concerning the position of Hoffmann La Roche in the market for vitamins, it was held that a market share of 47 per cent was, in one particular vitamin market, sufficient to establish dominance, whereas in other vitamin markets, market shares ranging between 18 per cent and 51 per cent were found by the Court not in themselves to constitute a factor sufficient to establish market dominance.

Example

In some cases a dominant position can exist even in a small market. In a decided case the Commission and the European Court found that there was a separate market for spare parts of a particular brand of cash registers since there was no other source of supply available in the UK.

Example

Conversely, in a recent judgment, the European Court rejected the Commission's finding that there was a separate market for the renting out and maintenance of telecommunications equipment, since contracts for the renting and maintenance of equipment could not be isolated as a separate market when users were free to choose whether to rent or to buy the equipment.

Example

A dominant position can exist in relation to a particular activity. A motor company which had the sole right to issue certificates of conformity in respect of imported motor vehicles required by Belgian legislation was found to have a dominant position since it had an exclusive right to issue those certificates in the supply of those services.

In any particular case it is a question of fact, depending on an analysis of the market as a whole and the position of a particular company in the specific market in question, as to whether there is a dominant position. It may, for example, be a defence to a charge of abusive dominance to establish that a market position is a result of advanced technical know-how or research and development capacity or marketing and advertising advantages which command consumer loyalty and not the result of foreclosure of the relevant market.

Abusive monopolisation

The European Court has stated that the concept of abuse is to be assessed by determining whether an undertaking in a dominant position 'has made use of the opportunities arising out of its dominant position in such a way as to reap trading benefits which it would not have reaped if there had been normal and sufficiently effective competition'.

Practices which may not otherwise be restrictive of competition may be abusive in a highly concentrated market since undertakings in a dominant position have to discharge the burden of proof that their dominance does not have the effect of impeding effective competition in the relevant market.

Article 86 of the Treaty of Rome contains a non-exclusive list of abusive practices. Examples of abusive behaviour from decided cases include:

Refusals to supply
- A refusal by an undertaking in a dominant position to supply another undertaking which may be economically dependent on the first undertaking.

In the IBM case, IBM was considered by the Commission to hold a dominant position (*inter alia*) in the supply of two key products for a particular computer system, and was found to have abused its dominant position by refusing to supply other manufacturers in sufficient time with technical information to permit the interfacing of those other products with IBM equipment, particularly by tying in the supply of IBM software and hardware and by discriminating between users of IBM software.

The Compagnie Luxembourgeoise, which had the exclusive right to operate Luxembourg television, behaved abusively by refusing to allow a particular undertaking broadcasting time for their advertising.

Excessive pricing

● A company in a dominant position which charges excessive prices for its products may be acting abusively. In one case the court confirmed the Commission's finding that there was evidence of abusive conduct where United Brands' prices in certain banana markets within the EC were excessive in relation to the economic value of the product supplied and differed considerably from one EC market to another.

Predatory pricing

● Akzo, the Dutch multinational chemical company, was found to have abused its dominant position in a particular chemical market by reducing its prices with the objective of driving out of business a competitor in the market in which it held a dominant position. The Commission emphasised in its decision that the selective nature of the price cuts, and the circumstances in which they were made, amounted to 'loss leader' tactics to make it impossible for the much smaller competitor in the market place to stay in business.

For the undertaking in a dominant position, valuable lessons are to be learned from these examples. It is particularly vulnerable to claims that it is acting abusively in a particular market, and must avoid discriminating between its competitors or using its market dominance in a manner which can be construed as unfair or intended to eliminate a competitor or competition. Conversely, those under attack from undertakings in dominant positions from other member states have valuable defences to attacking market dominant undertakings.

Price restrictions, market sharing and Articles 85 and 86: Examples of recent decisions

The Commission is vigilant in investigating, and severely punishes 'naked horizontal cartels' such as price fixing and market sharing and the abuse by groups with a dominant position in the market in any substantial area of the Community (Article 86). The following are recent examples of situations considered and action taken by the Commission:

Article 85 cases		
Name and reference	Situation	Action taken
Polypropylene (86/398)	Market-sharing and price-fixing system operated by 11 producers, including ICI and Shell. Regular 'bosses'' and 'experts'' meetings with unofficial directorate of the 'big four' largest companies.	Fines ranging from 10 million ecu to 500,000 ecu
Roofing Felt (86/399)	7 producers supplying 58 per cent of Belgian market, agreed minimum price list, ban on gifts to customers, market quotas and defensive measures to prevent import competition. Penalties for breaches, backed by a guarantee fund.	Fines ranging from 420,000 ecu to 15,000 ecu
Meldoc (86/596)	Agreement between 5 dairy companies producing 89.05 per cent of milk consumed in the Netherlands. Minimum price rules. Co-operation to resist market penetration from abroad. Concentration of sales in allocated territories. Quota system, supported by compensation payments. Committees and working parties.	Fines ranging from over 3 million ecu to 425,000 ecu
British Dental Trade Association (88/477)	Exhibitions of dental products: discriminatory rules and practices operated against non-UK producers and trade distributors. Also clauses restricting members from taking part in other exhibitions within stated times before and after BDTA exhibitions	BDTA fined 100,000 ecu. Rules modified by agreement with Commission: 85(3) exemption granted

Article 86 cases		
Name and reference	Situation	Action taken
Hilti (88/138)	Hilti abused its dominant position in EC in nail guns (power activated fastening tools) by tying sales of its cartridge magazines to sales of Hilti nails. Applied a range of pressures and sanctions to customers and importers, including unfair discounts and litigation. Hilti's 'safety requirement' defence was rejected.	Interim measures and fine of 6 million ecu
British Sugar (88/518)	British Sugar, with a monopoly in UK for beet sugar and 58 per cent market share for granulated sugar, abused its dominant position by attempting to stop sugar merchants Napier Brown re-packaging industrial sugar for retail sale. Measures included withholding supplies and offering special bonuses to Napier Brown's customers.	After threat of interim measures, fine of 3 million ecu (would have been larger but for British Sugar's subsequent good conduct and compliance programme)

Note: the rate of exchange of 1 ecu against the pound sterling on 1 October 1988 was approximately 1.52. Some of the above Commission decisions are subject to appeal to the European Court.

5. The practical application of EC competition policy

Developing a Community law reflex

Dual enforcement

EC competition rules are applied in two separate but related legal contexts. The Commission has the primary responsibility for enforcement of Articles 85 and 86. However, as with many Community rules, Articles 85 and 86 have what is known as 'direct effect' in the legal systems of member states; it is therefore open to any individual to invoke these rules and seek appropriate relief before their domestic courts. As a consequence the business must be conscious of this double perspective, whether it be to minimise exposure to EC competition rules or in order to decide how best to invoke the rules against competitors. In this sense a business must develop a Community law reflex in deciding in its 1992 strategy how it can best employ the EC competition rules.

EC competition rules and the Commission

Exposure and remedies

DG IV

The Commission is the administrative authority charged with the primary enforcement of Articles 85 and 86. In this sense it has a similar role to that of the Office of Fair Trading in relation to UK competition rules such as the Restrictive Trade Practices Act 1976, the Fair Trading Act 1973 and the Competition Act 1980, although in a number of respects and in particular in so far as the Commission has the power to take binding decisions, its powers are more extensive than the Office of Fair Trading. Community legislation bestows upon the Competition Directorate of the Commission (DG IV) wide powers of investigation, search of premises and seizure, and primary competence in the enforcement of Articles 85 and 86. UK businesses must therefore know how and when to deal with DG IV, and be aware of their exposure and potential remedies.

How to deal with the Commission

As previously stated, unless an agreement, arrangement or course of conduct which has a restrictive effect on competition does not have a perceptible effect on trade within the Community, it will fall to be considered under the EC competition rules. Before settling an agreement or starting out on a particular course of conduct, a number of fundamental factors have to be taken into consideration.

Discuss and review with DG IV

If there is any doubt as to whether a proposed course of action is consistent with the EC competition rules, you should, where appropriate with professional advisers, discuss the draft agreement or proposed arrangement with DG IV. The Commission practises an open door policy and is always prepared to review a draft agreement or arrangement internally with interested parties to determine its compatibility with Article 85. The Commission will often suggest how an agreement can be modified to bring it within the competition rules.

If in doubt, notify

If there is a possibility of the agreement falling within the prohibition in Article 85(1) and it is not covered by a block exemption, the agreement should be formally notified to the Commission. Although the process of notification inevitably involves time spent in preparation, the provision of substantial quantities of information, not to mention the incurring of legal fees, the advantages outweigh the disadvantages. The Commission can grant an exemption retroactively from the date of notification. The sooner an agreement is notified the longer the period of protection from fines is likely to be, since such protection does not exist for any period of operation of an agreement prior to notification. The Commission has exclusive competence to provide an exemption pursuant to Article 85(3) and, unless and until such exemption is given, the restrictions in the agreement which infringe Article 85(1) are provisionally void. The prescribed notification form A/B (other than in the air and maritime transport sectors) requests the Commission either to declare that the agreement does not fall within Article 85(1), which is known as a negative clearance, or to grant an exemption pursuant to Article 85(3). In granting an exemption the Commission can attach appropriate conditions to the operation of the agreement such as, for example, a requirement on the parties to notify the Commission as to the future operation of the agreement and/or review its operation prior to the expiry of the exemption, to limit the operation of the exemption for a specific period of time so as to enable the Commission to review its operation at some future date. The Commission may also require the parties to notify it of any other events which may be symptomatic of this operating in a restrictive manner: for example, any refusals to meet export orders, the joining of another party to the agreement or the supply of any trade information under an agreement.

In practical terms the main difficulty with individual exemptions is the time it may take the Commission to process a notification and grant exemptions. Since the object of an application for exemption is to secure the legal validity of an agreement, the exemption procedure is often unsatisfactory.

Alternatively seek a comfort letter

An alternative procedure which businesses are increasingly using, and which to a certain extent obviates some of the disadvantages of seeking an exemption or negative clearance, is to request the Commission to issue comfort letters. As the term suggests, these are letters from the Commission to notifying parties stating that the Commission does not believe that there is any need to take action in relation to the agreement or arrangement either because it falls outside Article 85(1) or because it may satisfy the requirements of Article 85(3), although in such a case the issue of a comfort letter does not amount to an exemption pursuant to Article 85(3). The practical effect of a comfort letter is to stop the Commission from changing its mind as to the status of the agreement unless there has been a material change of circumstances or unless the letter is written on the basis of incorrect information supplied by the parties. The precise status of comfort letters before national courts is, however, uncertain, although it would seem unlikely that a national court would consider it appropriate to find that an agreement infringed Article 85 if a comfort letter had been issued declaring otherwise. The issue of a comfort letter by the Commission ensures continued immunity from fines, since the agreement remains a notified agreement.

How to seek the protection of the Commission

Any company or firm that believes itself to be a victim of behaviour by its competitors which infringes EC competition rules can make a complaint to DG IV against the parties concerned. A number of factors may make such a course an appropriate means of achieving the most effective remedy.

Commission's power of obtaining information

The complainant may not know the precise details of the agreement or arrangement or conduct which is damaging its competitive interests in the market place. The Commission, however, has wide power to obtain information from the parties by making a formal request to supply information and/or documents within a specified period of time. The Commission can also impose penalties upon parties for failing to provide this information once the Commission has taken a formal decision requesting the information from the parties.

Commission's powers of investigation

The Commission can carry out all necessary investigations into undertakings having regard to any special features of a particular case. Sometimes this will be done in the form of a dawn raid; on other occasions it will provide the parties with advance warning of its intended visit. The European Court is about to decide the extent to which the Commission is entitled to seize documentation during the course of an investigation. It is clear, however, that failure on the part of the undertakings being investigated to produce the relevant documents to the Commission can render them liable to fines on a daily basis. Under its powers of investigation, the Commission can examine books and other business records of parties, take copies or extracts from the books and business records, ask for oral explanations on the spot and enter any premises, land or means of transport within EC territory belonging to the undertakings concerned. There is no right in Community law to have a lawyer present for such meetings, although normally the Commission will allow a limited time to elapse for the parties to acquire legal representation.

Dawn raid

Resolution and adjudication

Settling the case   It is not uncommon that, during the investigation phase of Commission procedures, there will be an amicable settlement of a dispute using the good offices of the Commission. This can often provide the most effective and speedy means of resolving a dispute. Settlement will often be accompanied by a Commission press release and a formal exchange of correspondence between the parties and the Commission.

Interim measures

In the event that the Commission considers that there is a strong *prima facie* case of infringement, and that there is a serious and urgent risk that irreparable harm will be caused to the party seeking relief or to the public interest, it can take an interim decision for the infringement to be bought to an end. The Commission has shown that it is able to act with relative speed under this procedure and has taken a variety of actions under it, including ordering a party to supply another party, refusing to allow undertakings to acquire further shares in a company in a takeover situation, ordering the cessation of predatory pricing and an order requiring the execution of a detailed supply agreement under which the Commission was to be notified of any price changes by the offending party or any case where it was unable to fulfil orders.

A good example of the practical operation of interim measures was the *Akzo* case. In that case Engineering and Chemicals Supplies Limited (ECS), a small producer of organic peroxides, alleged that the UK subsidiary of Akzo, a large Dutch multinational company, had abused its dominant position in the relevant market by implementing a policy of selective and below cost price-cutting designed to damage ECS's business and to exclude it as a competitor from the specialised sub-market in the flour additives sector in the UK and the Republic of Ireland. According to ECS this oppressive conduct by Akzo orginated in threats made at a meeting in 1979 between Akzo and ECS. In 1979 ECS obtained an injunction from the English High Court (see p. 72) but subsequently in 1982, when the conduct complained of appeared to continue, ECS made a complaint to the Commission which carried out an on-the-spot investigation at Akzo's premises in both the Netherlands and the UK. The Commission subsequently issued an interim measures decision which, amongst other things, required Akzo's UK subsidiary to return to the profit levels that it had been applying before the alleged threats were made and implemented.

The *Irish Distillers* case is another practical example of the operation of interim measures. The Commission's proposed interim measures took the form of requiring bidders not to purchase jointly or separately further shares in Irish Distillers unless the purchase was conditional on a favourable Commission decision under Article 85; the bidders were also required to refrain from exercising the votes attached to the shares already acquired.

Professional privilege and confidentiality

Variations in privilege

There are considerable differences in the laws of member states concerning the privileged status of communications between a client and his lawyer. It is clearly of the utmost importance to UK businesses to know in competition matters the status of communications with their lawyers, given the Commission's wide powers of investigation.

Community law acknowledges the principle of legal privilege. In the hotly contested litigation between AM&S Europe Limited and the Commission, the European Court decided that the Commission had the sole power to adjudicate on claims of privilege in relation to advice or other documentation passing between a lawyer and his client which may be examined by the Commission in investigations under the competition rules. It held that it was open to any aggrieved parties to challenge before the European Court a decision by the Commission ordering production of documents which a party considers are privileged, and the Court has power to grant interim measures to prevent disclosure of those documents to the Commission until the dispute on privilege is resolved.

However, all businesses must always bear in mind that in Community law privilege only attaches to communications with independent legal advisers and not with in-house Counsel. Therefore they must be vigilant to ensure that any advice or document-passing with legal advisers for which legal professional privilege may be sought at some stage is done with *external* legal advisers.

Confidentiality

Any information or documentation coming into the Commission's possession as a result of the exercise of their powers under the competition rules are covered by an obligation of professional secrecy. Moreover, any information the Commission obtains must be used exclusively for the purpose of the investigation for which it was acquired. When a complaint is made to the Commission, the Commission may or may not want to send a copy of the complaint to the other party. A complainant should establish with the Commission in advance whether it objects to disclosure of its complaint and the complainant should always be clear in advance as to any information which it wishes to remain confidential. It is possible to make a confidential complaint or include confidential annexes in complaints, although it is rare for the Commission to act on a complaint which is not disclosed to the other party.

The Commission's independent powers

Irrespective of whether an agreement or arrangement has been notified to the Commission or a complaint made, it is open to the Commission to launch its own investigation in relation to any agreement, practice or other activity which it may suspect infringes the competition rules. This general supervisory function of the Commission in competition matters by DG IV demonstrates further why the competition rules are all-embracing and cannot be circumvented or ignored by UK businesses in developing their 1992 commercial strategy.

Challenging Commission decisions before the European Court

There may be occasions on which a company feels aggrieved because a complaint to the Commission about the conduct of another company has been rejected. For example, a retailer may have been refused access to a selective distribution network on grounds which his lawyers advise the retailer are inadequate. Again, a company may have complained to the Commission that the conduct of a business competitor amounted to a breach of Article 85 or 86. In each case the Commission may have rejected the complaint and may also have granted an exemption to the company in respect of the conduct of which complaint has been made. Such decisions of the Commission may be challenged before the European Court, provided that the complainant company has been directly and adversely affected by the conduct of which complaint has been made. In order to secure the option of a judicial challenge to the Commission's determinations in such cases, a company would be well advised to complain formally to the Commission at the earliest opportunity, and to participate in the Commission's investigation, making submissions and offering evidence on the adverse effects on its business of the conduct of which complaint has been made. In these circumstances, the company would be entitled to challenge the Commission's decision to reject a complaint, or to grant an exemption. A number of cases of this kind have been initiated before the Court. For example, the proceedings in the *Philip Morris* case, which is of significance in the context of mergers and takeovers (see pp. 117–22), arose from the rejection by the Commission of a complaint by a cigarette manufacturer that certain agreements between two of its competitors were likely to restrict competition.

Remedies before the UK domestic courts

Since the EC competition rules apply directly in member states, private parties can invoke Articles 85 and 86 before their domestic courts. This may lead to a party claiming:

- That an agreement is void as infringing Article 85
- That an injunction should be granted to enforce the competition rules
- Damages for breach of the competition rules

Decisions of the domestic courts

Powers of exemption

Although only the Commission can grant an exemption pursuant to Article 85(3), the domestic courts are empowered to enjoin any party from infringing Article 85. It is therefore for the domestic courts to decide whether, in any particular case, the agreement does so clearly infringe Article 85 that an exemption is very unlikely to be granted by the Commission, even if it has been notified to the Commission, or whether there is no infringement of Article 85 and therefore the question of an exemption under Article 85(3) does not come into play.

Example

In a recent case before the English courts, an interim injunction was granted to prevent the enforcement of an agreement for the supply of juke boxes, pin tables and video game machines between a company which had taken over a number of tied public houses in the Humberside area and a number of those public houses. The agreement limited the persons who were permitted to supply the equipment to the public houses to those suppliers on an approved list, on which the plaintiff was not included. The High Court held that a restriction of this nature infringed Article 85(1) and could not benefit from a block exemption pursuant to Article 85(3) since the very clause in question was a black clause under the relevant EC block exemption for tied-house agreements. Therefore the judge concluded that the agreement should be treated as being in breach of Article 85(1) so that the machine suppliers could seek the Court's protection against the consequences of the company enforcing the agreements with its public house tenants.

Example

In the *Akzo* case, following a meeting between Akzo and ECS in November 1979 at which ECS claimed that it had been threatened that Akzo would decrease its prices below cost if necessary as a means of limiting ECS's ability to supply the market, ECS applied for and was granted an injunction under Article 86 of the EC Treaty in an *ex parte* application to the High Court in London. There followed a settlement in which Akzo undertook not to reduce its normal selling prices for the chemical in question in the UK or elsewhere with the intention of eliminating ECS's competitors and agreed to pay ECS's legal costs.

The recent Plessey/GEC litigation, in which Plessey sought an injunction to stop GEC posting its offer document on the basis that the Siemens/GEC bid for Plessey infringed EC competition rules, is a further example of the practical application of Articles 85 and 86 before the English courts.

Role of the Commission

Invariably an agreement which is the subject of legal proceedings under Articles 85 and 86 before the English Court will also be the subject of consideration before the Commission. In this situation the domestic court has the option either to adjudicate upon the dispute or to suspend the proceedings pending determination by the Commission. The European Court has held that national courts should allow proceedings to continue when they find the act complained of is clearly not capable of having an effect on competition or does not affect trade between member states or where there is no doubt that there is not an infringement of Article 85 and/or Article 86. The Commission actively encourages private parties to seek remedies before the national courts, and on occasions is prepared to indicate in writing its position to litigants before domestic courts on questions of EC competition law (although this is not binding on the domestic court).

Damages

English authorities suggest that damages are recoverable for breaches of the EC competition rules. The basis upon which damages may be claimed before domestic courts for breach of Articles 85 and 86 must be no less favourable than the damages recoverable for infringement of comparable provisions of domestic law.

The position as regards the recovery of damages in English law was reviewed by the House of Lords in the *Garden Cottage Foods* case. A company owned and run by Mr and Mrs Bunch carried on the business of purchase and resale of bulk butter. Between May 1980 and April 1982 the company purchased 90 per cent of its bulk butter requirements from the Milk Marketing Board and in turn resold the majority of this butter to a single Dutch customer. In March 1982 the Board informed the Bunchs' company that following a review of its sales and marketing strategy it had decided to limit the sale of bulk butter to four other distributors in England and Wales and that, in future, the company would have to purchase its bulk butter from other distributors. The company applied for an injunction against the Milk Marketing Board on the basis that its conduct infringed Article 86 of the Treaty of Rome. In order to decide whether to grant an injunction, the House of Lords had to decide whether damages were available for breach of Article 86 and whether that would, in the event of an injunction not being granted, be a satisfactory remedy. It decided that an individual citizen in the UK affected by a breach of Article 86 can bring an action for damages based on breach of statutory duty. Therefore, in determining whether damages will be a sufficient remedy or whether an injunction should be granted, the normal considerations of balance of convenience must apply.

Defamation

A further question that arises in this context is whether an English complaint to the Commission can result in defamation proceedings before the English courts for statements made in such a complaint.

The answer is that it cannot. In a case decided in 1984, the Court of Appeal held that a communication of this nature with the Commission is covered by absolute privilege and cannot form the basis of a defamation action before the English courts, since otherwise parties would not consider themselves free to communicate with the Commission for fear of being sued for defamation.

Community law as a sword

A company wishing to invoke EC competition rules to protect its position has to decide whether to invoke the assistance of the Commission in Brussels by way of complaint, to seek a remedy before the English courts, or both. In practical terms the following considerations should be taken into account:

- Do not shy away from your Community law remedies. Community competition laws have the same force and effect as all provisions of English law.

- Although the costs of litigating points of Community competition laws before the English courts should be no greater than litigating any other area of domestic law, significant savings may be made if the Commission route rather than the domestic route is taken because, compared to litigating before the English courts, making

Community law as sword and shield

a complaint to the Commission usually involves significantly less expense. The costs involved in making a complaint to the Commission are however generally unrecoverable. This must be set against possible delays in going the Commission route compared with the very speedy remedies available in seeking interlocutory relief before the English courts.

- Often there will not be sufficient evidence successfully to obtain an interlocutory injunction. However, through its powers of obtaining information and investigation, the Commission can often discover information which is otherwise difficult or impossible to obtain, which should enable it to substantiate whether there has been a breach of the competition rules which may otherwise go unremedied.

Community law as a shield

For any company whose business activities are likely to bring it into contact with the EC competition rules, the most effective means of protecting its position in relation to EC competition rules is to adopt a policy of 'forewarned is forearmed'. The likelihood of fines and the serious consequences as regards enforceability of agreements, possible injunctive relief and damages create a considerable incentive to the

Compliance

institution of an EC competition law compliance programme. While there are costs involved in the creation of such a programme, the costs of fines on dealing with a full-scale investigation which may follow a violation of the competition rules make the institution of an anti-trust compliance programme a prudent commercial course.

The essence of any such compliance programme is for businesses to identify all areas of commercial activity which bring them into contact with competitive situations. It may be within the context of a trade association, it may be in the context of customer or marketing relations or commercial relations generally with competitors. It is vital that all relevant personnel

Documentation

are identified from the outset, since any investigation by the Commission or discovery in the course of domestic litigation may unearth documents at all levels of personnel whether on the marketing, purchasing or manufacturing side of a particular business. At the very basis of a compliance programme is a document retention policy which should avoid the need to retain unnecessary documents and ensures that any document which may be relevant to a competition investigation is identifiable and ascertainable within its proper context by the company.

In recent decisions the Commission has emphasised that the creation of a compliance programme goes some way towards mitigating fines on the case as heard. It is evidence of a wish to comply with Community competition rules.

6. Growth in partnership – marketing concepts and methods

The importance of a 1992 outlook

An EC marketing strategy

It is important to approach marketing strategy within the EC with a single market outlook. A US company marketing products in the USA would not normally seek to confine sales by its purchasers to certain regions of the country or try to impose or maintain price differentials on a geographical basis, other than those reflecting increased distribution costs (or if it did, the US anti-trust authorities would be concerned to stop it). While it has been illegal since 1962 to divide the Common Market into watertight national markets by such means as export bans and the restrictive use of trademark rights, the advent of 1992 makes such an approach even more of an anachronism.

When planning an EC marketing strategy a business should, therefore, begin with the concept of the single market and only seek to impose restrictions on distributors and licensees (or on itself) if it is commercially essential to do so. Agreements planned with this approach are much less likely to fall foul of Article 85 or, if they do, should stand a better chance of being eligible to benefit from a block or individual exemption.

The conversations opposite between three marketing directors illustrate the type of practical issues which businesses grapple with on a daily basis and how Community competition rules are of relevance to those issues.

A business seeking to market its products within the EC is likely to consider one or more of the following distribution systems:

- Exclusive distribution
- Exclusive purchasing
- Selective distribution
- Franchising
- Sales agencies

Marketing director of a toy company

'We have just renewed our agreement with our exclusive Spanish agent. He keeps minimum stocks of our toys, orders his requirements from us monthly and pays by irrevocable letter of credit. We have made sure that his agreement does not allow him to export our products outside Spain as this would upset our other markets in the EC, particularly France and West Germany, where our products sell at higher prices and we have to protect the interests of our local distributors.'

The director is making the classic mistake of confusing agents and distributors. His 'agent' in Spain is in fact a distributor because he buys and resells to his own customer and takes the commercial risk. The absolute ban on exporting toys outside Spain is a serious breach of Article 85. It would be permissible under the exclusive distribution block exemption to require the distributor not to pursue an active sales policy outside Spain but he must not be prevented from exporting toys to buyers who approach him from other EC countries – as may well happen until the price differential levels off.

Marketing director of a computer manufacturer

'Our Italian subsidiary markets our computers through a network of authorised dealers who have to satisfy us that they have the expertise and facilities to advise customers and give them an after-sales service. Our policy is not to appoint more than one dealer for each 10,000 of population.'

The company is operating a selective distribution system. It is in breach of Article 85 because of the policy of restricting the number of dealers according to population. All suitably qualified dealers must be admitted to the system. However, if there is a strong enough commercial justification for this extra restriction, the company may succeed if it applies to the Commission for an individual exemption or comfort letter.

Marketing director of a manufacturer of sailing equipment

'We chose the franchise route to expand our market for our sailing equipment and clothing in France through a network of franchised shops using our name and logo. The operation is supervised by our main distributor in France who has been appointed as our master franchisee.'

The company will be able to take advantage of the block exemption for franchise agreements, which allows the territorial restrictions normally associated with franchising, if it can show that substantial know-how is being communicated to franchisees so as to give them a competitive advantage and the availability of commercial or technical assistance during the life of the agreement.

This section deals with aspects of EC competition law in this area most likely to be of immediate interest to businesses. We also highlight some of the comparative advantages and pitfalls which will be relevant in those cases where it is feasible to choose between more than one marketing strategy.

Exclusive distribution

The block exemptions

The advantages to the consumer of exclusive distribution agreements have long been recognised under EC competition law as justifying the anti-competitive restrictions which they entail. These normally include the allocation of a territory to the distributor in which the distributor is granted exclusive selling rights while undertaking not to deal in competing products or to promote sales of the contract products outside his allotted territory. The block exemption for such agreements, in force since 1967, was superseded in 1983 by the current Regulation and its companion for exclusive purchasing agreements, which also covers tied public houses and solus petrol service stations.

These block exemptions provide a well defined legal framework and have great practical importance. The Commission estimates that there are over 100,000 exclusive distribution agreements and over 500,000 exclusive purchasing agreements in the Community. Thanks to the block exemptions, these agreements generate relatively little administrative work for the Commission, which only becomes involved in special circumstances, such as certifying agreements as being in conformity with the block exemptions, helping parties to amend non-conforming notified agreements and pursuing agreements with clauses prohibited under Article 85(1) where this is considered to be in the public interest.

Permitted restrictions

Under the block exemption for exclusive distribution agreements the only restrictions on competition which may be imposed are:

- On the supplier, an obligation not to supply the contract goods to resellers or users in the contract territory

- On the exclusive distributor, the obligations not to manufacture or distribute competing goods; to obtain contract goods for resale only from the supplier; and to refrain, outside the contract territory and in relation to the contract goods, from seeking customers, establishing any branch and maintaining any distribution depot ('active sales')

The supplier is also allowed to require the distributor to undertake obligations designed to provide an efficient distribution system and promote sales, such as purchasing complete ranges of goods, advertising, maintaining stocks and providing guarantee services.

Parallel trading

Price differentials

Parallel imports and exports are the life-blood of EC competition. Parallel traders, operating independently of the manufacturer's official distribution channels, buy goods in areas of the EC where they are cheap and sell them cheaply where they are expensive, with the result that the higher prices tend to be forced down to competitive levels.

While the supplier is allowed to impose a restriction on active sales by the distributor outside his territory, it is a serious breach of Article 85 to prevent or impede the flow of parallel imports and exports of the contract goods both in the distributor's territory and in other parts of the Community. The block exemption will not apply if the supplier seeks to ban the distributor from exporting the goods by way of unsolicited ('passive') sales, or to prevent intermediaries or users (by the use of trademark or other industrial property rights, for example) from obtaining the goods from other dealers inside the community (or from outside if there is no other available source of supply). Also, the block exemption does not apply if the exclusive distributor is, in fact, the only source of supply of the contract goods in its allotted territory.

Recent decisions show the seriousness with which the Commission regards attempts to impede the flow of parallel imports and exports. The Italian subsidiary of the Swiss Sandoz Group, for example, was fined 800,000 ecu for printing, over a period of many years, the words 'export prohibited' on its sales invoices for pharmaceuticals; Tippex was fined 400,000 ecu for making strenuous efforts through its agreements with distributors and concerted practices to 'cut out the parallel market'; and a fine of 300,000 ecu was imposed on Quaker Oats for the pressure applied by its toy division, Fisher-Price, to prevent a buying group in Northern Ireland from supplying three of its members in the Republic of Ireland so as to force them to purchase from Fisher-

Price's Irish distributor at a substantially higher price. Attempts to control the prices charged by distributors are similarly prohibited under Article 85(1).

Agreements between competitors

The exclusive distribution block exemption does not apply where manufacturers of identical or equivalent goods enter into reciprocal exclusive distribution agreements, or a non-reciprocal exclusive distribution agreement, unless the total annual turnover of one of the parties does not exceed 100 million ecu.

Exclusive purchasing

The block exemptions for exclusive distribution and exclusive purchasing are in many respects similar. Both are concerned with an exclusive agreement between two parties with a view to the resale of goods.

The main difference is that, under an exclusive purchasing agreement, the reseller is not allotted an exclusive territory in which its sales effort must be concentrated in return for protection against competition from other resellers who buy direct from the same supplier. While agreeing to buy all its requirements of the contract goods from the supplier, the tied reseller is free to decide where to make its sales effort. For its part, the supplier is free (unless it agrees not to do so) to supply other resellers in the sales area where the tied reseller operates, at the same level of distribution.

Selective distribution

Approved dealers

A system of selective distribution is one where the supplier selects the dealers he is prepared to supply ('approved dealers') and imposes a restriction preventing them reselling to anyone except end users or other approved dealers. The improved distribution and provision of specialist after-sales service resulting from selective distribution are acknowledged by the European Court and the Commission to outweigh the anti-competitive effect of prohibiting sales to non-appointed dealers and other restrictions on the commercial freedom of manufacturers and traders. So far only the motor vehicle industry has the benefit of a block exemption regulation for selective distribution. Otherwise, the extent to which the provisions of selective distribution agreements fall outside Article 85(1) or, alternatively, can qualify for individual exemption under Article 85(3), is governed by a series of decisions of the Court and the Commission.

Conditions avoiding infringement

A selective distribution system is held not to infringe Article 85 only if it meets the following conditions:

- Approved dealers must be chosen on the basis of objective criteria which relate to the technical qualifications of the dealer and his staff and the suitability of his trading premises. Such conditions must be laid down uniformly for all potential dealers and must not be applied in a discriminatory fashion.

- These criteria must be 'reasonably necessary' to ensure adequate distribution of the goods (the Commission has, for example, expressed doubt as to whether plumbing fittings could be considered as sufficiently technically advanced products to justify a selective distribution system).

- All suitably qualified dealers must be admitted to the system.

- Suppliers must not take any measures likely to obstruct parallel imports.

Even if these conditions are met, it is likely that Article 85(1) will be broken (and unlikely that exemption under Article 85(3) will be granted) if any of the following occurs:

- The selective distribution system has taken over the entire market in the goods

- The result is a rigid price structure not outweighed by other competitive advantages

- The agreement contains requirements relating to sales promotion, such as an obligation for the dealer to maintain stocks or achieve a specified minimum turnover

- Guarantees which a manufacturer of consumer durables offers as part of its after-sales service are not valid throughout the Community and honoured by all selective distributors, regardless of the country in which the product was purchased

Honouring product guarantees

With regard to the last point, it is important for businesses to be aware that, irrespective of the form of distribution adopted, refusal to honour a guarantee in respect of a product which has not been imported or exported through a manufacturer's established network may constitute a substantial barrier to trade and an infringement of Article 85.

In November 1986, the Commission issued a specific warning that, unless consumers could obtain Community-wide guarantees, the distribution agreements covering such products might be declared incompatible with the competition rules.

Sony's guarantee system

As an example of what should be done, Sony has introduced a new guarantee system for its electronic games to ensure that its guarantee conditions are applicable without discrimination in each member state to all Sony products, irrespective of the place of purchase within the EC:

- Sony undertakes to repair or replace defective parts without charging for labour or parts, subject to presentation of the guarantee card

- The guarantee is honoured by all Sony subsidiaries and their approved repairers and resellers in the Community, regardless of the member state in which the product was purchased

- The conditions of the Sony guarantee are those applicable in the country where the after-sales service is requested under the guarantee; this applies particularly to the guarantee period, which is not necessarily the same throughout the Community

Franchising

Franchising consists essentially in exploiting intangible property rights (trademarks or names and know-how) for the purpose of selling goods or providing services in premises of uniform appearance and with the same business methods. Franchise systems normally improve the distribution of goods and/or provision of services. They provide franchisors with a means of rapid and effective market entry through a uniform sales network, with limited investment. It is thus particularly suitable for small and medium-sized business and increases inter-brand competition. Franchising also allows independent traders to set up outlets more rapidly and with a better chance of success than if they had to do so without the franchisor's experience and assistance and are thus able to compete more effectively with large undertakings such as department stores and supermarkets. Consumers benefit from the maintenance of a high and consistent standard of quality associated with the franchise network.

In the leading case of *Pronuptia*, decided in 1986, the Court took a positive view of franchising and held the agreement in that case to be, in most respects, free of anti-competitive restrictions, even though many of the clauses in the agreement would have been held to infringe Article 85(1) in the context of a selective distribution agreement.

The evaluation of franchising in *Pronuptia* has been followed in a number of decisions by the Commission, and in a block exemption Regulation adopted at the end of 1988, which came into force on 1 February 1989.

Definition of franchise

In the Regulation, a franchise is defined as a package of industrial or intellectual property rights relating to trademarks, trade names, shop signs, etc., to be exploited for the resale of goods or the provision of services to end users and which includes at least:

- The use of a common name or sign and a uniform presentation of contract premises and/or means of transport

- The communication by the franchisor to the franchisee of secret substantial marketing and sales know-how capable of conferring a competitive advantage on the latter

- The continuing provision by the franchisor to the franchisee of commercial or technical assistance during the life of the agreement

Advantages of franchising over selective distribution

Although selective distribution and franchising are not identical, in some cases the relationship of a manufacturer with its selective distributors is very similar to that of a franchisor with its franchisees and this may give businesses an opportunity, in appropriate cases, to structure their marketing arrangements as a franchising system rather than a selective distribution system. The advantage of doing so will be that Article 85(1) is not infringed by any of the following, which would require (and would not necessarily receive) specific exemption in the case of a selective distribution agreement:

- Discretionary choice by the franchisor of his franchisees, without any obligation to admit them automatically if they have the necessary technical qualifications and suitable premises

- The application of franchising to products which are not 'technically advanced'

- Promotional requirements such as an obligation to maintain stocks or sell minimum quantities

An obligation on the part of the franchisee to exploit the franchise only from the contract premises, or on the part of the franchisor to refrain from exploiting the franchise or selling goods and services under a similar formula in an area allocated to the franchisee, is covered by the block exemption.

Permitted restrictions on the franchise

Guarantees

The permitted range of restrictions which are not treated as anti-competitive consists of those which are designed either to protect the franchisor's know-how so that the franchisor can communicate its knowledge to the franchisees and provide them with the necessary assistance in putting its methods into effect, without running the risk that this know-how and assistance will, even indirectly, aid its competitors, or to preserve the identity and reputation of the franchise network. It is a condition of the exemption that the franchisee must honour guarantees for goods bearing the franchisor's trademark even though they may have been supplied by other franchisees and this condition is, therefore, the same for franchise agreements as for selective distribution agreements.

Franchisee's alternative sources of supply

A block exempted franchise agreement must leave the franchisee free:

- To purchase the franchised goods from other franchisees or from the franchisor's own authorised distributors.

- To obtain supplies of goods 'of equivalent quality to those offered by the franchisor'. This applies only to goods which are incidentally used or sold in the franchisee's business, as opposed to the basic product with which the franchised name and reputation are identified. Taking the case of a franchised hamburger bar, for example, a franchisor might insist on being the exclusive source of supply of the meat for the hamburgers but not of the tableware.

These conditions will have to be considered carefully where the franchisor's profit is to come from the supply of goods or materials to its franchisees rather than from royalties.

Other features

The exemption will extend to the typical international franchising structure, under which a master franchisee is appointed for a given territory where it grants and operates a series of sub-franchising agreements.

- The franchisor may recommend, but must not fix or restrict, the franchisee's resale prices

- The franchisee may be prevented from selling goods competing with the franchised products (but may not be restricted with regard to spare parts or accessories)

- The franchisee must not be prevented from supplying any end user because of his place of residence

- The franchisee must indicate its status as an independent trader, although not so as to interfere with the common identity of the franchised network

- The franchisee cannot be prevented from continuing to use the franchisor's know-how after termination of the agreement, where it has fallen into the public domain otherwise than as a result of the franchisee's own action

Sales agencies

Control of sales agents

The appointment of sales agents is the fourth route a business may choose for the marketing of its products in the EC. If agents are truly

**Application of
Article 85**

acting as agents and not as independent traders they will, in economic terms, be no more than an arm of the business they represent so that Article 85 will not apply to the contract appointing them. The agent can therefore be required to work exclusively for the principal and the principal can appoint the agent as sole agent for the territory, without the need to apply for negative clearance or exemption under Article 85(3).

In appropriate cases, therefore, a business will be able to exercise considerably greater control over marketing strategy, including export sales and prices, if the company is represented by sales agents rather than independent distributors.

Christmas Message

This will not work if the agent is in reality functioning as an independent trader, irrespective of what the agent is called in the contract. In its so-called 'Christmas Message' notice of 24 December 1962, the Commission laid down guidelines for the treatment of exclusive agency contracts made with 'commercial agents', emphasising that the key test of an agent is that they must not, either under the contract or in practice, assume any of the financial risks associated with the sales they negotiate – for example, maintaining substantial stocks, providing substantial service to customers or determining prices or business terms. Agency will not, therefore, be available as a marketing route where a free after-sales service is required at the agent's expense.

Sales agents and business risks

The issue of an updated version of the 'Christmas Message' was one of the Commission's unfulfilled competition policy objectives for 1988. New guidelines are needed because doubts have been cast by case law as to whether Article 85 applies where the agent:

- Trades on his own account in goods which are the same as or similar to those covered by the agency

- Trades in such goods for another principal

- Trades on his own account or for another principal, in any goods

In April 1987, a personal view on this from the head of the Commission's Competition Directorate was published, indicating that he did not think an agency falling outside Article 85(1) was restricted to cases where the agent acted for one principal only and that attention should, in his view, be focused on the principal–agent relationship rather than the agent's other activities. The decisive factor was whether, on an economic analysis of the principal–agent relationship, the financial risks were carried by the agent or the principal.

There is support for this view in the Commission's decision in December 1987 in *ARG/Unipart* where the Commission analysed the division of responsibilities and risks between Unipart and its former holding company, Austin Rover. The Commission held that Unipart was acting in the role of Austin Rover's agent, and was therefore outside Article 85 with respect to Austin Rover branded parts, the sale of which Unipart had undertaken to promote for Austin Rover's account and for a commission. At the same time Unipart had assumed entrepreneurial risks, therefore acting as an independent trader subject to Article 85, for other categories of parts.

Economic analysis of the division of risks is, therefore, likely to be a central feature of the Commission's updated notice and it is to be hoped that this time it will refer to the position of all agents, not merely commercial agents as in 1962.

The protection of commercial agents

Businesses which have appointed sales agents in Common Market countries, or which are considering doing so, should be aware of the Directive of 18 December 1986 'On the coordination of the laws of the member states relating to self-employed commercial agents'. The UK does not, unlike most other member states, have specific laws for the regulation of agency agreements and the protection of commercial agents, whereas there is a wide variety of such provisions in the laws of the other member states.

UK derogation The Directive requires all the member states to change the domestic laws relating to self-employed commercial agents so as to comply with its provisions by not later than 1 January 1990. This date is extended to 1994 for the Republic of Ireland and the UK, and (for the compensation provisions only) to 1993 for Italy. Agreements already in existence when the new legislation comes into force will have to be made subject to the new rules not later than 1 January 1994. The UK government is expected to announce its proposals for legislation to comply with the Directive in the near future.

A commercial agent is defined as a self-employed intermediary who has continuing authority to negotiate the sale or the purchase of goods on behalf of another person (the principal), or to negotiate and conclude such transactions on behalf of and in the name of that principal.

Indemnity The Directive requires member states to enact measures for indemnity or compensation of commercial agents after termination of their agency contracts, in one of two alternative ways. Under the first, the commercial agent would be entitled to claim indemnity for the benefit to the principal of the goodwill built up and the agent's loss of commission on future contracts, not to exceed one year's average commission calculated over the previous five years (or the life of the agreement, if shorter). Under the second alternative, the agent would be entitled to compensation for damage suffered as a result of termination of relations with the principal, particularly where the agent can show loss of the opportunity of earning further commission whereas the principal benefits from the business the agent has generated, or of amortising costs and expenses which the agent incurred on the principal's advice. It will not be possible to agree in advance to exclude the new compensation provisions and they will apply even when the agency contract is terminated because of the agent's death or on grounds of age, infirmity or illness or circumstances where the agent could not reasonably be required to continue his activities.

The Directive also lays down requirements for minimum periods of notice, calculation and payment of commission, agreement formalities and other details of the principal–agent relationship and restraint of trade clauses, which may be valid for not more than two years after termination of the agency contract. The text of the Directive and (when available) legislative proposals of the member states should be considered before agency agreements are entered into or varied.

The varied operation and effect of the rules for the protection of distributors and agents in certain member states is illustrated on pp. 151–7.

7.   Growth in partnership – licensing

The purpose and value of licensing

The licensing of intellectual property rights – patents, trademarks, copyright and know-how – can occur in many contexts, for example as a feature of a joint venture, where it is the effect on competition of the arrangements as a whole which will be relevant for the purposes of EC competition law. In this chapter we are concerned with the case where a company wishes to penetrate the market in one or more EC countries more quickly with the help of local enterprise and also to avoid the time lag and capital investment required in expanding manufacturing capacity, or setting up local capacity. In return, the company will receive a royalty and, in some cases, may also derive profits from the supply of essential materials or ingredients.

Technology transfer
Conversely, the licensee may, by taking a licence, get a head start on its competitors through a transfer of technology developed by the efforts and research and development expenditure of the licensor, or the advantage of being able to sell its goods under a trademark already carrying the goodwill of the licensor's reputation and benefiting from its previous marketing and advertising.

Often licences relate to more than one type of intellectual property right: for example, a licence under a trademark calling for the
Safeguarding standards
observance by the licensee of the licensor's standards of quality to protect its goodwill may well involve substantial transfers of know-how in the course of inspection visits of technicians to the licensee's factory. This may also occur in the context of patent or design copyright licences, and such licences and know-how agreements may in turn give the licensee the right, or the obligation, to sell the finished product under the licensor's trademark.

Although it is the Commission's declared policy to encourage licensing as a means of co-operation for more rapid technology transfer and development with a view to the ultimate benefits to competition and the consumer, the rules as to what is and is not regarded as anti-competitive, and what may qualify for exemption, are extremely detailed and complex; and it is foolhardy for companies to embark on the granting or taking of licences without the benefit of expert legal

**The licence
negotiator**

advice. While a 1992 outlook will undoubtedly be very helpful to the negotiator of licences within the EC, as it is in the case of marketing strategy, this will not be enough; and the purpose of this chapter is to give the negotiator a broad view of the main competition and single market considerations which underlie the detailed rules.

Intellectual property rights under Community law

The ownership of a patent for an invention, a trademark in respect of a name or other mark and of copyright in its various categories gives the owner a form of monopoly to those rights exercisable for their periods of validity. Know-how affords much weaker protection as its value depends upon the information being kept secret from competitors and on the duty of a licensee to maintain confidentiality. The ability of a know-how licence agreement to stand up in law will therefore be of paramount importance.

**Moribund
restrictions**

In the past it was customary for owners of intellectual property rights to impose on their licensees a long list of restrictions, including territorial exclusivity and non-competition clauses; some of these are now illegal under Community law.

Community law insists that, in the licensing and enforcement of intellectual property rights within the EC, two rules must be observed:

- These rights must not be used as barriers to obstruct the free movement of goods across EC frontiers once the goods have been lawfully placed on the market

- No anti-competitive restrictions likely to affect trade between member states may be included, unless they can be justified by benefits to the economy and the consumer

Free movement of goods

Article 30

The principle of free movement of goods is laid down in Article 30 of the Treaty of Rome. It is qualified by a saving clause for the protection of 'industrial and commercial property' such as patents and know-how, so long as these are not 'a means of arbitrary discrimination or a disguised restriction on trade between member states'.

Community law interprets these words to mean that the Treaty of Rome protects the existence of intellectual property rights but limits their exercise. Only the 'specific subject matter' of each type of right is protected and the right is exhausted once a product has been placed on the market by the owner or the owner's licensee. Once particular goods have been lawfully marketed, no use may be made of the ownership of a series of parallel rights in other countries, such as patent or trademark registrations, to prevent the free circulation of the particular goods after their first sale within the EC.

No anti-competitive restrictions

Typically, licence agreements used to include restrictions binding the licensor and licensee on the following lines:

- An undertaking by the licensor not to manufacture or sell the product in the licensed territory or to license others to do so

- An undertaking by the licensee not to manufacture or use the product outside the territory

- An undertaking by the licensee not to export outside the territory

- An undertaking by the licensee not to deal in competing products or engage in competing activities in the territory (or, possibly, anywhere in the world)

- Mutual obligations for the parties to do their best to prevent third parties from exporting or importing the licensed products into or out of the licensed territory (although in fact the licensor could achieve this merely by owning parallel patents, trademarks and copyright in other member states)

Such terms were not thought to be unreasonable because a licensor was free not to grant any licence at all and could therefore dictate its terms for doing so.

Protection of investment

All these restrictions will, except in special circumstances, infringe Article 85(1) but may be exempted under Article 85(3) provided that certain modifications are made to allow room for competition which will not prejudice the interests of the licensor and licensee. In recent years there has been a growing realisation on the part of the European Court and, to a lesser extent, the Commission, of the importance to businesses of being able to protect their research and development costs and investment in plant or marketing by appropriate exclusivity provisions and other restrictions. Without these the investment might not have been made or licences not granted, to the detriment of the consumer and competition within the Community as a whole.

The block exemptions

The most important guidelines for businesses negotiating licence agreements are to be found in the block exemptions under the Regulation for patent licences and the Regulation, adopted at the end of 1988 and which came into force on 1 April 1989, for know-how licences.

These block exemptions attempt to strike a balance between the legitimate interests of licensor and licensee which require protection for the sake of encouraging cooperation and stimulating competition as against the need to preserve competition. The Commission is intent on not allowing the block exemptions to be used as a breach through which genuinely uncompetitive agreements can be driven; and a clause-by-clause approach is adopted, because the Commission does not have the advantage of knowing the facts and market background of the particular agreement. Where the Commission does have this knowledge because an application is made for individual exemption or a comfort letter, experience shows that, within reasonable limits, they will be responsive to special commercial needs and ready to enter into a dialogue which should result in a commercially acceptable agreement.

General approach

The approach of the licence negotiator should therefore be as follows:

- When dealing with a patent or know-how licence, to bring the terms within the block exemptions if possible

- In the case of a trademark or copyright licence, where there are no block exemptions, to make the terms conform with the principles underlying the patent and know-how block exemptions so far as applicable

- To seek the Commission's informal advice insofar as it is commercially necessary to include terms not falling within the patent or know-how exemptions, or in respect of any trademark or copyright licence with exclusivity or other clauses which would otherwise infringe Article 85 and, after establishing what will be acceptable, to notify the agreements formally and obtain comfort letters

Because of the time factor in a particular case, it may be necessary to sign an agreement with a condition that it (or any restrictions which it contains) will not come into effect until the Commission's comfort letter has been obtained or, alternatively, undertaking to make any changes which the Commission requires, with the option for either party to terminate the agreement if the requirements are not acceptable. If a comfort letter is obtained, it will be unlikely in practice that the agreement will be challenged in the national courts or made the subject of a successful complaint to the Commission.

Examples of clauses regarded as not normally infringing Article 85 (or given exemption under the know-how and patent block exemptions, provided the other requisites of those regulations are met) are clauses to protect the secrecy of know-how; to prohibit sub-licences or assignments without consent; to ban the licensee from using the relevant intellectual property right after termination of the agreement; mutual and reciprocal exchange of non-exclusive rights regarding improvements; reasonable provisions for quality control and inspection in the case of patents, know-how and trademarks; a requirement for patent and know-how licensees to mark the licensed goods with the licensor's trademark (provided that this is not used to bolster up a market sharing or market dividing arrangement); and a requirement for the licensor to grant the licensee any more favourable terms which the licensor may grant to another undertaking after the agreement is entered into. Such provisions are regarded either as being inherent in the rights themselves (as in the case of the secrecy of know-how) or unobjectionable from the point of view of their effect on competition within the EC.

The 1992 licence negotiator

It is beyond the scope of this book to attempt to analyse in detail the decisions of the European Court and the Commission regarding the licensing of intellectual property, or the terms of the block exemption regulations for patent and know-how licence agreements. However, in many cases, businesses will be called on to negotiate, at the pre-contract stage, the terms for granting an intellectual property licence. We therefore give some broad guidelines as to the approach to negotiating a licence which is most likely to produce a formula which will correspond with the parameters with which lawyers will invariably have to work when the licence comes into their hands.

Identify the subject-matter

Identify at the outset what rights you are licensing and their relative importance – patents, know-how, copyright and trademarks. For example, an agreement presented as a trademark licence with provisions for inspection and control of quality often turns out to involve a substantial amount of transfer of know-how or design copyright as in the case, for example, of a garment manufacturer which licenses its designs for manufacture under its trademark. This may be of considerable importance because, while there is no block exemption covering trademark licences, the know-how block exemption does cover agreements with ancillary clauses relating to trademarks and other intellectual property rights, which may be made subject to the same permitted restrictions as the know-how.

Know-how procedures

In the case of a know-how licence it will be necessary to identify the know-how transferred in a separate document or to record it in some other form existing at the time of transfer. Where the know-how is communicated on a day-to-day basis orally between technicians it will be necessary to make detailed notes of visits and transfers between technicians, identifying the know-how imparted, and to keep notes on a central file which will have to be returned on the expiry of the agreement.

Period and exclusivity

Keep the period of the agreement as short as is consistent with your commercial interests. This particularly applies to the period in which the rights granted by the licensor are to be exclusive to the licensee and for which restrictions on the licensee may be imposed. There may be cases where payment of royalties and other provisions of the agreement may be allowed to continue after the life of the relevant right if this is to facilitate payment by the licensee over a longer period.

There are detailed rules in the patent and know-how block exemptions about the types of territorial exclusivity clauses which are exempted and the maximum periods from which they may operate. The detailed requirements under each regulation are different and must be carefully observed. The following general principles may be noted.

- Restrictions must not, unless justified by special circumstances, continue in force after the licensed intellectual property right has expired. The life of know-how is treated as ending when it ceases to be secret or 'substantial' (broadly, of importance to the relevant process, product, or service). Territorial exclusivity for know-how must not be for more than ten years from the first licensing of the technology in the licensed territory or (where clauses protecting the territorial exclusivity of other licensees are concerned) in the EC.

- The Commission tends to take a more lenient view of restrictions designed to protect the exclusivity of the territories of the licensor and the licensee than of those which are intended to provide exclusivity for other licensees. In the latter case, a stricter rule is applied in order to avoid the Common Market from being divided up into water-tight compartments impervious to competition. The general rule is that such restrictions may not be imposed at all for exports to a member state where there is no present licensee (or which is not reserved as part of the licensor's territory), and must keep open the possibility for the licensee to accept unsolicited orders to export to those territories, as opposed to actively promoting sales there.

  The patent and know-how block exemptions do, however, allow the licensor to impose an absolute ban on exports to the territories of other licensees for a maximum period which must not exceed five years from (in the case of know-how) the first licensing of the technology in the EC or (in the case of patent) the first marketing in the EC of the patented product.

- In a pure trademark licence it is unlikely that the Commission will ever sanction an absolute ban on exports to protect the territories of other licensees. To stand a chance of getting exemption or a comfort letter, the licensee's obligation should not go beyond refraining from pursuing an active sales policy or putting the licensed product on the market in territories of other licensees or distributors of the licensor, or reserved to the licensor. A restriction on these lines was exempted in the case of *Campari* (decided in 1978 and so far the only reported case of a trademark licence exemption). However, as already stated, different considerations will apply where the trademark is only a subsidiary feature of an agreement where patents or know-how are the main subject matter.

'No challenge' clauses

Avoid 'no challenge' clauses under which the licensee undertakes not to dispute the validity of the licensed patents, copyright or trademark or the secrecy of the know-how. The Commission takes an extremely serious view of such clauses and has imposed heavy fines for including them. However, the patent and know-how block exemptions allow the licensor to have the right to terminate the agreement if the licensee challenges validity, and a similar attitude will probably be adopted in the case of copyright or trademark agreements for which exemption or a comfort letter is sought.

Undertakings not to compete

Avoid undertakings by either party not to compete – whether between the two parties to the agreement or with other companies, and relating to any aspect of business within the Common Market such as research and development, production or use of competing products and their distribution. However, the know-how block exemption allows the licensor the sanctions of terminating the licensee's exclusivity, ceasing to communicate improvements in the event of the licensee engaging in competing activities, and requiring the licensee to prove that the licensed know-how is not being used for production of unlicensed goods and services. Inclusion of a similar clause in the context of patents, trademarks or copyright is likely to be viewed favourably by the Commission.

Royalties

The following general rules may be helpful as a starting point, although there is probably more scope in the area of royalties than any other to persuade the Commission that the commercial circumstances justify special treatment.

- Where royalty is based on turnover, it should be calculated only by reference to the product for which the licensed intellectual property rights are used and not products outside the licence. An exception will, however, be allowed where the number or value of the items is difficult to establish separately from a larger unit in which they are incorporated, or where there is no separate market for the licensed product.

- There is no objection to providing for a minimum royalty, or for a fixed sum payable by instalments.

- Under the patent and know-how block exemptions, the parties may, to facilitate payment by the licensee, spread royalty payments over a period extending beyond the life of the patent or the entry of the know-how into the public domain.

- Apart from these special exceptions, royalties must not be payable after the right which is the subject of the licence has ceased to exist (though, in the case of know-how, if it ceases to be secret through the fault of the licensee, royalties may continue to be enforced for the duration of the agreement).

As yet there is no guidance regarding royalty provisions in trademark licences. Intrinsically there seems to be no reason why royalties should not continue to be payable for so long as the licensee wishes to continue to use the licensor's trademark, which will continue in force for so long as the licensor cares to renew it. However, the agreement will be reviewed as a whole to see whether it has an effect which is restrictive on competition and this may well be the case if, for example, the agreement is for a long fixed period without a right to break on the part of the licensee, combined with an obligation to pay a substantial minimum royalty.

Other clauses

The following is a brief note of other clauses commonly found in licence agreements which should be omitted or modified to avoid infringing Article 85.

Parallel imports and exports

There must be no question of either party having a duty to block parallel imports or exports (see pp. 79–80).

Tying

The licensee must not be required to accept unwanted ties, such as licences under other processes or the purchase of other goods or services, unless these are necessary for a technically satisfactory exploitation of the licensed technology, or to maintain the quality standards observed by the licensor and other licensees.

Market sharing

The licensee must not be restricted in its choice of customers, forms of distribution or (with the aim of sharing customers) types of packaging. However, the licensee may be prevented from using secret know-how to construct manufacturing facilities for third parties.

The quantities the licensee may manufacture or sell must not be limited, except that the licensee may be required to limit manufacture to its own products and to sell the licensed product only as an integral part of or as a replacement part for its own products.

The block exemption for know-how agreements enables the Commission to allow, using an accelerated procedure, customer and quantity restrictions in order to provide a second source of supply to a particular customer.

Price fixing

Neither party may be restricted on the determination of prices or discounts.

Post-term use ban   During the life of a patent or the continued secrecy of know-how or, presumably, the continued validity of copyright or a trademark, the licensee may be required to cease using the rights after the termination of the agreement, and no fixed time limit is prescribed. However, a post-term use ban cannot prevent a licensee using practical experience gained from working an expired patent.

Improvements   An obligation of the licensee to grant non-exclusive licences for improvements to the licensor is permitted by the know-how and patent block exemptions, provided that the obligation is reciprocal. The know-how block exemption spells out that that licensor's obligation must be of the same duration as that of the licensee if there is a post-term use and the improvement know-how is inseparable from the licensor's know-how. If the effect of a grant of improvements is to prolong the duration of the agreement, it must be open to the licensee to refuse the improvements or 'break' the agreement at the end of the initial period and thereafter at not less than three-yearly intervals in the case of the know-how exemption (annually after expiry of the last of the original licensed patents, where the patent exemption is relied on).

A case study on the know-how block exemption

Since 1892 Deadweight Plc, an iron foundry, has manufactured Coveritt manhole covers of superior quality, using a secret technique first conceived by the founder of the company, Herbert Coveritt. The technique was never patented but has remained secret. Deadweight has since produced a steady flow of improvements, as a result of which its products have remained competitive and have achieved a significant market share in the UK and West Germany.

For many years, licences have been granted to manufacturers in other European countries and elsewhere and all these licences require the licensee to sell the product under the Coveritt trademark. Although the trademark gives a selling advantage, the most important benefit is access to Deadweight's evolving technology and experience.

Deadweight's licences are for periods of ten years. Deadweight undertakes not to manufacture or sell Coveritt manhole covers in the territories of its licensees who, in turn, agree not to manufacture or sell the covers in the UK or West Germany, which are reserved to Deadweight, or to manufacture them or actively promote their sales in territories allocated to other licensees.

Deadweight now wishes to grant a ten-year licence on these terms to a new licensee in France, and wishes to know whether the agreement is permitted under the know-how block exemption regulation.

The know-how block exemption allows periods of territorial exclusivity of ten years from the date of the first licensing in the EC of 'the same technology' – this means the technology as licensed to the first licensee and enhanced by any improvements made subsequently, irrespective of whether and to what extent these improvements are exploited by the parties or other licensees and irrespective of whether there is patent protection in any member state. Accordingly, Deadweight's lawyers advise that, regardless of the value of the improvements, the block exemption will not apply to the proposed licence

---

and that Deadweight should, therefore, make an application to the Commission for individual exemption. Deadweight succeeds in convincing the Commission that the extent and importance of the improvements justifies a period of mutual territorial exclusivity but the Commission decides that, as this is not a new and advanced technology, ten years is too long. A comfort letter for a five-year period is issued.

In 1983, Deadweight developed (but did not patent) a new technology for lining pits for the disposal of nuclear waste. In 1985 it granted know-how licences for its process in the USA and Australia. In 1989 it proposes to grant its first licences in the EC to a French and an Italian company to exploit the process in their respective countries. The licence agreement is to be for ten years, with clauses for the protection of territorial exclusivity as described above.

As there has been no previous licence for this technology in the Common Market and the know-how is still secret and important, Deadweight's licences will be covered for the full ten-year period of territorial exclusivity by the know-how block exemption regulation (provided that the other rules are met) and no individual application to the Commission is necessary.

The block exemption also allows Deadweight to impose an absolute ban for up to five years on its licensees on marketing the pit linings in Italy and France respectively, even in response to unsolicited inquiries. However, they must remain free to export to member states not reserved to Deadweight, or licensed to third parties.

8. Growth in partnership – co-operation, joint ventures and information exchange

Co-operation and competition

Trojan horses

The Commission has repeatedly stated its desire to encourage cross-frontier co-operation and joint ventures, with benefits such as promotion of innovation, speedier transfer of new technology, development of new markets and an increase in the number of businesses competing within the Community. On the other hand, it is determined not to allow such arrangements to be Trojan horses for anti-competitive cartels 'leading to market sharing, raising of barriers to entry and the intensification of market power'. A co-operation agreement or joint venture infringes Article 85 if it may appreciably affect inter-state trade and its object or effect is to prevent, restrict or distort competition. It may be exempted under Article 85(3) if it contributes to improving production or distribution of goods or promoting technical or economic progress while allowing consumers a fair share of the resulting benefit. Such exemptions are particularly likely to be forthcoming if the participating businesses are small or medium-sized enterprises, although joint ventures between companies with very substantial market shares are also frequently approved.

Permitted co-operation agreements

The Commission's policy

In 1968 the Commission responded to requests from industry to indicate its view of the application of the competition rules to co-operation between enterprises by issuing a formal Notice. This Notice had no legal effect, but gave practical advice on the view the Commission was likely to take of certain types of agreement. The Notice welcomed co-operation between small and medium-sized enterprises where such co-operation enabled them to work together more rationally and increase their competitiveness on a larger market. The Commission added that co-operation among large enterprises could also be economically justifiable without presenting difficulties from the point of view of competition.

Such arrangements as joint market research, and the joint execution of research work up to the stage of industrial application, were stated to be compatible with Article 85(1), provided that participating companies did not restrict their freedom of action. However, the Commission took a practical view of the effect of such restrictions in assessing their compatibility with the competition rules. If the effect of a joint research and development (R&D) agreement was that the parties no longer conducted independent research and development, this would be enough to attract the application of Article 85(1) and the agreement would be to that extent prohibited unless Article 85(3) applied. Also, the Commission has taken the view that pure R&D agreements involving no restrictions on the behaviour of the parties may nevertheless be caught by Article 85(1) where the R&D is central to developing the market in question and the market is oligopolistic in structure.

R&D

In 1985 the Commission issued a block exemption on the application of Article 85(3) to R&D agreements. The Commission noted that, in certain circumstances, such as where the parties agree not to carry out other research and development in the same field, these agreements might infringe Article 85(1). Such agreements might however be exempted under Article 85(3), since co-operation in R&D work and in the exploitation of the results generally promotes technical and economic progress, which in turn benefits consumers through the introduction of new and improved products. This would be the case where an R&D programme and its objective are clearly defined and each of the parties is given the opportunity of exploiting any of the results that are of interest to it, or where the results are used solely for the purposes of further research. An agreement between two or more competing manufacturers whose combined market share exceeds 20 per cent of the market for the appropriate products in the EC or a substantial part of it would not however be exempted under the 1985 block exemption (though it might benefit from an individual exemption).

Specialisation agreements

Manufacturing companies with a large output enjoy the advantages of economies of scale. Indeed those who drew up the blue-print for the Common Market in the 1956 Spaak Report sought to make available to Europeans those advantages so long enjoyed by US manufacturers in the USA's single market. One way in which companies can simultaneously achieve economies of scale and concentrate upon a shorter product range is through a specialisation agreement. For example, two companies each manufacturing a number of different components might each agree to stop manufacturing certain lines and purchase all their requirements in that range from the other party to the agreement. To the extent that the companies are actual or potential competitors, the agreement will restrict competition and, if there is an effect on inter-state trade (which there is likely to be unless production is insignificant), there will be a breach of Article 85(1). The agreement will also restrict competition by limiting the selling opportunities of other producers of the components subject to the exclusive purchasing commitment.

However, specialisation agreements are regarded by the Commission as improving the production and distribution of goods, because participating enterprises can concentrate on the manufacture of certain products and thus operate more efficiently, and supply their products more cheaply. As long as competition prevails on the relevant market, consumers will receive a fair share of the resulting benefit. The currently applicable block exemption Regulation, issued by the Commission in 1985, exempts specialisation agreements coupled with exclusive purchasing conditions subject to certain conditions. In particular, the block exemption will not apply automatically to agreements between parties whose relevant aggregated market share exceeds 20 per cent of the relevant product market in the EC or a substantial part of it, and whose aggregate annual turnover exceeds 500 million ecu. Companies with a larger turnover but with less than a 20 per cent market share may, however, benefit from an opposition procedure (see p. 59).

Joint ventures

A joint venture goes further than co-operation, in that generally a new business entity is created, but falls short of a full merger of the parents, who remain independent. There is no standard definition of a joint venture. Its essential features can be described as an integration of operations between two or more separate firms, resulting in an enterprise under the joint control of entirely independent parents, to which each parent makes a substantial contribution and which exists as a separate business entity. A joint venture which is not a disguised cartel will create significant new enterprise capability such as new production capacity, new technology, a new product or entry into a new market. The most usual form of joint venture is a jointly owned company whose activities and sphere of operations are defined by a series of agreements and industrial property licences, but a company is not essential if the agreements between the parties result in a separate, jointly controlled business entity.

Joint Venture

Can a joint venture qualify for clearance?

Consistently with its policy of encouraging joint ventures, the Commission has been increasingly liberal in granting individual exemptions under Article 85(3). It would, however, be of much greater value to the business community if firm criteria were established for types of joint venture which are not regarded as anti-competitive by nature and which are therefore likely to qualify for negative clearance by the Commission. Exemption under 85(3) has the disadvantage that, during the long delay before a decision is made, the terms of an agreement which infringe 85(1) will be unenforceable in the national courts and the Commission may well ask the parties to re-negotiate terms of the joint venture at a time when the commercial balance has changed (for example, after the most important technology and know-how have been imparted and the new business established).

In deciding whether a joint venture falls outside Article 85, the basic question is whether the parties to a joint venture are competitors or potential competitors. If they are, the formation of the joint ventures is inherently likely to restrict competition between them (even in the absence of explicit contractual provisions) because the presence of competition would jeopardise the value of the parent companies' investments. Also, the existence of the joint venture in one field is **Spillover effect** likely to lead to the so called 'spillover effect' of providing 'opportunities and inducements' for the parent companies to extend their common activities to related interests in other areas.

To obtain negative clearance, therefore, it has to be shown that the parent companies are not competitors or potential competitors. The Commission identifies as a crucial factor 'whether taking into account all relevant economic circumstances, the parties could reasonably be **Market entry** expected to enter the market individually. If individual market entry is unlikely in the foreseeable future, the joint venture will not restrict existing competition but will lead rather to the creation of new competition.'

The Commission has not granted a negative clearance under Article 85(1) for a joint venture for many years. However, in recent decisions there is the beginning of a welcome new trend towards greater readiness on the part of the Commission to hold that parties to a joint venture are not competitors or potential competitors although, in all the cases in question, negative clearance was not given because of the detailed terms and other circumstances (individual exemption under Article 85(3) was granted instead).

In one of these cases, Corning, an American company which had developed optical glass fibres, entered into joint ventures with BICC, Plessey and other major cable manufacturers. The Commission found that the parties had not been actual or potential competitors, because Corning had experience in optical cable manufacture while its partners had no experience in glass manufacture which could have led to a competitive invention. Neither was likely to enter into the market of the other as part of a natural and foreseeable extension of its business activity. The co-operation was, therefore, complementary and did not give rise to a restriction or distortion of competition. However, Article 85(1) was held to apply because the joint ventures with several cable companies formed a network potentially restricting competition.

Can a joint venture be exempted?

The Commission has also shown greater flexibility and readiness, given economic justification, to sanction joint ventures which in substance restrict competition between major competitors. For example, in a joint venture between Olivetti and Canon a key factor was that an agreement restricting competition brought a substantial transfer of advanced technology into the EC as a *quid pro quo* for restricting competition in low and mid-range photocopiers and fax machines. In another case involving Enichem and ICI, the crisis created by structural over-capacity in the PVC industry was accepted as justifying a joint venture where these two very large companies co-operated with regard to R&D, manufacture and marketing through the joint venture as a fundamental step towards rationalisation.

In another striking case, the Commission exempted a joint venture between the Ford and Fiat groups, the object of which was to take over the production and sale of Ford's Cargo Line heavy vehicles and to begin marketing a range of heavy vehicles manufactured by Iveco, a Fiat group company, to supplement the Cargo Line. Later, when Iveco's planned new generation of heavy vehicles replaced the Cargo Line, the joint venture was to market the entire range of Iveco heavy vehicles in the UK. In spite of the market-partitioning resulting from this agreement and its accompanying restrictions, the joint venture was exempted because of the need, not satisfied by Ford's Cargo Line, for manufacturers to sell a complete range of heavy vehicles to enable customers to take advantage of uniform maintenance and spare parts systems and the benefit of a 'rationalised and smooth transition from the old range of models to a new generation of vehicles'.

Joint sales ventures

Joint ventures formed solely for the purpose of joint marketing and sales are unlikely to receive exemption, although joint marketing may be accepted by the Commission as one of the elements in an exempted joint venture if the economy and the consumer can be shown to benefit. In one such case (*Floral*) where exemption was refused, the three largest French manufacturers of compound fertilisers, accounting for more than two-thirds of French production, and 10 per cent of Community production, formed a joint subsidiary for the purpose of selling their fertiliser in West Germany. The three companies sold their products at different prices to the joint subsidiary, but the subsidiary resold them on the West German market at the same price. Other terms of sale were also identical. The parties only notified the arrangements after the Commission commenced investigation of their activities. The parties argued that the effect of the joint venture was to promote their exports to West Germany, and pointed out that the arrangement had brought about an increase in penetration of the West German market. They also argued that the joint use of the subsidiary's distribution network saved distribution costs.

The Commission found that the arrangement restricted competition, affected inter-state trade and could not be exempted. It restricted competition since, even in the absence of an express agreement not to export to West Germany independently of the joint subsidiary, this was the practical effect of concerting sales policy through the subsidiary. The parents would hardly compete with their subsidiary. There was an effect on inter-state trade, since the joint venture regulated exports from France to West Germany. The Commission rejected the argument that, since exports by the French companies amounted to only 2 per cent of West German consumption, the effect on competition and trade was insignificant. The market was dominated by a handful of large operators, and the arrangement in question simply had the effect of tightening this oligopoly. By contrast, even relatively small quantities could, if put on the market individually, have an appreciable effect on market conditions.

The Commission could find no redeeming features which would merit the grant of an exemption. The joint sales venture had brought no advantages in distribution which could not have been achieved by the parties acting independently. They were perfectly capable of making direct sales in competition with each other on the West German market. In any event, consumers had secured no advantage through a reduction in prices on the West German market, since the joint subsidiary's pricing policy had not had the effect of reducing prices on the West German market. The Commission fined the participating companies.

Exchanges of information

The pitfalls of information exchange

Co-operation involves the exchange of information; and business executives constantly meet their opposite numbers from other companies at conferences, seminars and industry-related committees. It is vital for businesses to be aware that to supply confidential business information to competitors, whether directly or by an indirect route such as a trade association, may be in breach of Article 85. This is a developing area of Community law with many grey areas, and one should therefore err on the side of caution when deciding whether Article 85 is likely to be infringed in a particular case.

Companies should therefore make sure, as part of their EC competition compliance programme, that their executives are made aware of the dangers of Article 85 and are warned to avoid disclosing confidential information of the type described in this section.

What is wrong with exchanging information?

Effect on market behaviour

Article 85 does not prevent a company from reacting intelligently and adapting its prices and other terms of business to the actual or anticipated conduct of its competitors, provided all determine their policies independently. Community law treats independence as lost if competitors, or potential competitors, arm one another with secret business information which makes it possible for them to co-ordinate the market behaviour of their companies. The exchange of information enables each company to identify and predict the other's competitive behaviour more precisely, quickly and easily than would otherwise be possible and thus reduces the uncertainty and risk which are fundamental to healthy competition. It also tends to create a climate in which prices and quotas are likely to be fixed, even if this is done by the parties independently and not by agreement.

It is therefore illegal for competitors, or potential competitors, to place at one another's disposal, directly or indirectly, confidential figures and other information such as prices, discounts or other terms of trade, sales figures, production quantities, production costs, distribution costs, budgets, and information on customers and future investment or marketing plans.

It is an aggravating factor if executives hold regular meetings to pass over the information. Such meetings provide their companies with a forum for raising criticism if inroads are made into their respective market shares or if the balance of power in the market is upset.

The market background to information exchange

The Commission pays particular attention to the structure of the market and has commented that 'the tendency of firms to fall in line with the behaviour of their competitors is particularly strong in oligopolistic markets', (i.e. markets characterised by the presence of a small number of relatively large suppliers). In such markets, the intensity of competition is reduced because the improved knowledge of market conditions aimed at by information agreements strengthens the connection between the companies concerned, so that they are able to react more rapidly and efficiently to one another's actions.

It is not necessary to show that actual restriction or distortion of competition has taken place as a result of the exchange of information. The restrictive effects on competition are treated by the Commission as inherent, though they may not be measurable or even apparent to an observer of the market unaware of the arrangement.

Example

The *Fatty Acids* case

These principles were applied in a recent case when the Commission considered an agreement between Unilever, Henkel and a subsidiary of Petrofina, whose combined market share for the supply of the fatty acids oleine and stearine in Europe was about 60 per cent.

Against a background of a market suffering from over-capacity and low or stagnant growth rates with declining profits and margins, Unilever was about to reduce its production capacity and the parties were concerned that the volatile market should not be de-stabilised by aggressive competition to secure the capacity which Unilever was about to give up.

Under the agreement, the parties disclosed to one another their annual tonnages for sales in Europe in the preceding three years so as to establish their then existing market shares, followed by similar figures on a quarterly basis, to enable them to monitor possible major changes in their relative positions.

The Commission held that the agreement was in breach of Article 85 and imposed fines of 50,000 ecu on each company, making it clear that the low level of the fines was due only to the fact that this was the first decided case where fines were imposed for a 'pure' information agreement where there was no proof of other anti-competitive activities.

Anonymous statistics for business studies

The Commission has stated that there is no objection to the supply of business information for the preparation of statistics by trade associations or reporting agencies, provided that it is not possible to identify the figures for individual businesses from the resultant compilations. Particular care is needed where figures are broken down into detailed categories such as country, product or period. It goes without saying that appropriate precautions should be taken to ensure that the trade association and its committee members themselves maintain total confidentiality.

Common industry standards

In 1987 the Commission added a second type of information arrangement to the permitted category, namely the exchange of technical and market information to provide a common industry standard. Nine computer manufacturers formed an association under the name 'X/Open Group' and entered into an agreement with AT&T, designed to increase the portability of computer programs between different machines, by creating an 'open industry standard' consisting of a stable but evolving common application environment for software based on a specified AT&T interface definition.

The Group published the *X/Open Portability Guide*, listing the interfaces belonging to the common application environment, and a software catalogue available to the public without restriction. There was no requirement for the Group members or others to adopt the standard, but there were obvious advantages, both for independent vendors and end-users. The agreement involved the exchange of technical and market information. The market information related to the European software industry and its requirements and to the structure of the market for the relevant AT&T operating systems, but excluded information relating to the products of the individual Group members such as prices, customers, market positions and production plans.

The Commission did not consider that the exchange either of the technical or the market information between the Group members affected their freedom to determine their market behaviour independently, and therefore ruled that, in this respect, there was no restriction of competition under Article 85(1). It went on to decide that certain criteria and rules for admission to membership of the Group were potentially discriminatory and therefore anti-competitive but it granted exemption under Article 85(3) because of the benefits to technical progress and consumers, which outweighed any distortions of competition.

Because of the danger that the Commission will find anti-competitive elements even in an information agreement of this type, such agreements should either be notified to the Commission, as was done by the members of X/Open Group, or discussed with the Commission and informally approved in draft before signature.

It should not be assumed that product or technical standard agreements will always escape Article 85 or qualify for exemption: the computer market is highly competitive and the Commission's approach may well be different in the context of an oligopolistic market like that for fatty acids (see above), or of an industry which lacks new technology.

Planning ahead

Despite the Commission's policy of encouraging cross-border co-operation agreements, joint ventures and exchanges of technical information, they remain essentially vulnerable to EC competition law. The uncertainty and expense of contested Article 85 proceedings can be avoided, or at least limited, by careful preparatory analysis and planning. Before embarking on negotiations where there is any possibility of an EC dimension, business executives and their advisers should carry out a thorough review of the EC consequences, so that the structure chosen and the presentation of the agreements in their economic context are most likely to be viewed in a favourable light by the Community authorities.

9. Growth by acquisition – takeovers and mergers

Before the *Philip Morris* judgment of the European Court in November 1987, the possibility of intervention at EC level was likely to affect only mergers involving the very largest companies. Now that the Court has ruled that agreements the purpose of which is the acquisition of total or partial ownership of enterprises by merger, acquisition or reorganisation may be subject to Article 85, the prospect of investigation by the Commission or of a 'Euro-defence' to a takeover bid has become a matter of much wider concern. In addition, multinationals and large companies may need to reappraise their plans for expansion by cross-border acquisition and merger in the light of EC competition policy if the long-debated Draft Merger Regulation is finally approved in 1989.

For these reasons it is important for business executives and their financial and legal advisers to be aware of the current state of development and the likely future direction of EC merger control. We therefore begin with a survey of the background, history and present scope of Article 85 and 86 as applied to mergers, followed by a summary and critical appraisal of the Draft Merger Regulation.

Background to EC merger policy

Forms of merger

Growth by acquisition may take many forms: the purchase of a publicly held company's shares by a recommended offer or by contested takeover bid, or the acquisition of shares or business assets by private agreement (in either case for cash or by way of share exchange); merger through the medium of a holding company which acquires the merging companies or their assets; and, in France and certain other member states, merger by 'fusion' whereby a company loses its identity and is absorbed, with its assets and liabilities, into the

Concentration

new concern. For convenience, the word 'merger' is used in this chapter for all forms of merger, acquisition and takeover, whether they involve acquisition of controlling or of minority interests in shares or assets. 'Concentration', the word normally used in EC competition law parlance, can be confusing as it is given two different meanings: sometimes it covers mergers in the wide sense described above, and sometimes it is confined to those which bring about a change of control.

Why EC competition policy needs merger control

Mergers may lead to economies of scale, increasing economic efficiency as well as creating business units of the necessary size and strength to compete on equal terms with the largest companies outside the Community. However, an effective competition policy needs power to control mergers because of the serious damage they may inflict on competition. In the words of the preamble to the Draft Merger Regulation discussed below:

> The dismantling of internal frontiers can be expected to result in major corporate reorganisations in the Community, particularly in the form of concentrations . . . Such a development must be welcomed as being in line with the requirements of dynamic competition and liable to strengthen the competitiveness of European industry, to improve the conditions of growth and raise the standard of living in the Community . . . It must be ensured that the process of reorganisation does not give rise to lasting damage to competition [and] the system of undistorted competition must therefore include provisions governing those concentrations which may impede effective competition in the common market.

Dominance situation

Mergers may damage competition in two distinct situations, labelled for convenience in this chapter 'dominance situations' and 'cartel situations'. A dominance situation may be brought about where one company gains control over a competitor, reducing the number of remaining competitors able to act independently and increasing the level of concentration within an industry. The internal structure of the two companies which thereby become a single economic unit has changed. Loss of competition may be particularly marked where the merger is horizontal (i.e. the companies are competitors in the same product market and at the same level of production or distribution).

Cartel situation

A cartel situation may occur where two independent competitors create a framework more likely to encourage co-operation than competition between them (for example if one company acquires a minority or 50 per cent shareholding in a subsidiary of the other). Regardless of whether or not there is an actual agreement to co-operate, the psychological effects of joint ownership and the mutual access to confidential information which is likely to follow may influence the mutual competitive behaviour of the parent companies and thus distort competition.

Auction rings

A cartel situation may also arise through the creation of a consortium of companies to engage in a takeover bid, if this results in an 'auction ring' effect so as to prevent the price of the shares in the target company from being driven up by the competing bids of the participants. Such a consortium may also be anti-competitive at the level of the product market if it involves an agreement to divide up the brands or other assets of the target company, or will lead to a permanent joint venture in the target company likely to encourage co-operation rather than competition. The *Irish Distillers* case (see pp. 158–65) is an excellent example of a consortium at both levels.

Market structures

In all these cases, the economic structure of the market will be crucial. Competition in a market with few suppliers, none of them controlling the market but each relatively large (oligopoly) is much more likely to be distorted if one of those suppliers takes over or acquires an interest in another, than in a market characterised by fierce competition among many suppliers. The sensitivity of a market to changes brought about by acquisitions and mergers is likely to be all the greater where the market itself is stagnant and without perceived prospects of overall growth in consumer demand. In such cases, growth may have to be achieved by acquisition of established rival brands or companies, with the result that competition suffers without the justification of compensating benefits to the consumer.

As an illustration, the computer market in the EC is characterised by the presence of many very large companies but is still highly competitive. This may be contrasted with the markets for cigarettes and spirits, where overall consumer demand is unlikely to expand significantly and collaboration between the few major suppliers is likely to have a direct effect on competition and on the flow of inter-state trade.

The inadequate tools for EC merger control

A system for the scrutiny and control of mergers should be designed to cause minimum interference with the efficient operation of the capital markets. It should produce quick and clear decisions before each merger is completed and should not require a reference to more than

EC inadequacies

one authority. For historical reasons, the control of mergers at Community level has fallen lamentably short of these objectives.

The development of a system of merger control in the EC has suffered from the lack of any specific provision for such powers in the Treaty of Rome; the European Court has attempted to make good this shortcoming through case law. Two judgments of the Court, *Continental Can* (1973) and *Philip Morris* (1987), are of cardinal importance. In *Continental Can*, the Court ruled that a company which already held a dominant position in the Common Market could be treated as exploiting it abusively so as to infringe Article 86, if it strengthened its dominance by taking over a competitor. In *Philip Morris*, the Court established that, contrary to previous thinking, Article 85 could apply to agreements the purpose of which was the acquisition of total or partial ownership of enterprises by merger, acquisition or reorganisation. (For convenience these are described in this chapter as share transactions, but the same rules apply to the acquisition of assets.)

Articles 85 and 86 were designed to attack anti-competitive agreements and abusive monopolisation and were not drafted with merger control in mind. Their application to mergers therefore tends to lead to uncertainty and instability instead of providing the orderly framework and timetable essential for the conduct of public share acquisitions and takeover bids.

Merger Regulation

Because the interpretation of Article 86 in *Continental Can* only gave the Commission power to control the *strengthening* of a dominant position as opposed to its *creation*, the Commission in the same year tabled a Regulation to give the Commission comprehensive powers to authorise and control major EC mergers with a significant cross-border element. Since 1973 the Commission has striven without success to persuade the Council of Ministers to adopt such a Regulation, which would require a unanimous vote. Its efforts were revived and intensified in 1988 and, following a proposal made at the beginning of that year, a working paper was circulated in July and an amended proposal, submitted in November, was published in the Official Journal in January 1989. Although there is now a general consensus as to the need for such a Regulation, agreement has not, at the time of writing, yet been reached on fundamentals such as the size thresholds which will bring a merger within the scope of the Regulation, or the relationship of competition laws and other approval requirements at Community and national level.

Restraining dominance: Article 86 and *Continental Can*

In 1966 the Commission issued a 'Memorandum on Concentrations'. The Memorandum concluded that the prohibition against anti-competitive agreements in Article 85 could not apply to agreements whose purpose was the acquisition of total or partial ownership of enterprises or of their assets. Conversely, a company which already held a dominant position in the Common Market could be treated as exploiting it abusively so as to infringe Article 86, if it moved significantly towards monopoly by taking over a competitor.

The Commission's controversial interpretation of Article 86 was adopted in 1973 by the European Court in the *Continental Can* case. Continental Can, the US packaging giant, was an internationally important manufacturer of metal packages, packing materials and packaging machines. Its recently acquired West German subsidiary had a high market share in that country in cans for preserved meat, fish and shellfish and in metal caps for glass jars. Using another subsidiary, Continental Can agreed to purchase a controlling interest in its Dutch licensee which was the largest manufacturer of metal containers in Benelux. The Commission ruled, firstly, that Continental Can had, through its West German subsidiary, acquired a dominant position in a substantial part of the Common Market and, secondly, that to acquire the Dutch company was an abuse of that position under Article 86. The effect was to strengthen Continental Can's dominance to the point where competition was practically eliminated.

Continental Can appealed to the European Court. The Court overruled the Commission's decision because it had failed to base it on a thorough market analysis. But at the same time, the Court confirmed the principle that acquisitions which strengthen a dominant position in the Common Market or a substantial part of it – in this case, West Germany – can amount to an abuse under Article 86 of the Treaty of Rome if the effect is to make any serious chance of competition practically impossible. It would be pointless, the Court said, to control restrictive agreements under Article 85, if undertakings were at liberty to eliminate competition altogether through merger. The Court remarked that 'such diversity of legal treatment could open a breach in the whole system of competition law that could jeopardise the proper functioning of the Common Market'. As Voltaire might have put it, 'As the Treaty of Rome did not provide a system of merger control, it was necessary to invent one!'

Under Community law the scope of Article 86 is wide enough to cover any merger which strengthens the dominant position of an undertaking in (or in a substantial part of) the EC, irrespective of the country where the company is established, or of whether it has a subsidiary located in the EC. The *Continental Can* case was itself concerned with the West German subsidiary of a US company. Where there is no EC subsidiary, the 'effects doctrine' under which Community law exercises jurisdiction over acts done outside the EC and having anti-competitive effects within the EC, may be applied, although this could give rise to problems of enforcement.

Widening the scope of Article 86

Since *Continental Can*, the Commission has not made any formal decision applying Article 86 to a merger. It has investigated a number of cases but has only threatened to use its powers on two occasions, when it succeeded in persuading the parties to abandon or limit the scope of their merger.

Meanwhile, since 1973, the threshold of what amounts to dominance under Article 86 has been widened by a series of European Court decisions, not as such concerned with mergers but, according to the Commission, equally applicable to them. In *Continental Can* the Court said that the degree of dominance reached must be shown to have 'substantially fettered' competition, so that only undertakings remained in the market whose behaviour depended on the dominant group. The Court has also interpreted abuse less strictly. Instead of having to prove substantial fettering of competition, it is probably now enough for the Commission to show that competition has already been *weakened* by the presence of the dominant undertaking and that some further action on its part would impede the maintenance or development of the effective competition in (or in a substantial part of) the Common Market.

Can more than one company jointly have, and abuse, a dominant position?

Shared dominance

Article 86 covers the activities of 'one or more undertakings' and in 1985 Commissioner Peter Sutherland said that the implications of shared dominance were being examined. In the following year, the Commission carried out a study of the concept of shared dominance and its relevance to competition policy and concluded that the two essential features of shared dominance were:

- The fact that a small number of enterprises account for most of the turnover in the market in question without any single enterprise having a dominant position

- A high degree of interdependence among the decisions of the enterprises

So-called tacit collusion may arise from the fact that members of an oligopoly become aware of their interdependence and of the probably unfavourable consequences of adopting a competitive attitude. The Commission applied its theory at the end of 1988 when it imposed large fines on three Italian flat-grass producers. However, there is as yet no decision of the European Court on shared dominance. In particular, it is not clear whether an abuse would require joint action or, in the case of a merger, whether it would be sufficient for a single company in the group to acquire a competitor.

Why Article 86 is unsuitable for merger control

Article 86 is inherently unsuitable for the control of mergers. It applies only to the strengthening, not to the creation of a dominant position; its scope is wide and uncertain and depends on Commission policy statements and annual reports instead of properly reported cases (there has been no formal decision since *Continental Can*); and it has no machinery for authorising mergers beneficial to the consumer on the lines of Article 85(3).

If and when an EC Merger Regulation is adopted, the Commission may well tend to treat its merger control powers under Article 86 as a dead letter. But the Commission's attitude will not alter the fact that Article 86 remains part of Community law, enforceable in the national courts at the instance of anyone aggrieved by a merger which falls outside the scope of the Regulation.

Restraining cartels: Article 85 and *Philip Morris*

Why Article 85 is unsuitable for merger control

Those engaged in takeover bids and other share transactions require a merger approval system with a structured procedure and timetable, which Article 85 does not provide.

Unlike Article 86, Article 85 does have a system for notifying agreements to the Commission and applying for exemption on grounds of pro-consumer and other benefits (see Chapter 4), but a decision may take several years.

Article 85 also provides that the anti-competitive agreements which it prohibits are automatically null and void and are thus unenforceable in the national courts. If an agreement is notified and later exempted, it will be treated as valid (and will also have the benefit of exemption from fines) as from the date of notification. If, on the other hand, an agreement is not notified until after a merger has been completed, then even if the Commission later grants exemption under Article 85(3) the original merger agreement and transfer of shares will, arguably, still be null and void under Article 85(2) as applied by the national laws of the member states concerned.

To avoid such a catastrophe, if a company's advisers consider that there is any risk, however remote, of Article 85 applying, advance notification of the merger agreement or offer to shareholders will be essential. This is unfortunate as it may well lead to the Commission being swamped with protective notifications.

Lastly, when the Commission grants an exemption to an anti-competitive agreement on grounds of its advantages to the consumer under Article 85(3), the exemption has to be for a limited period, after which it comes up for review. To impose a time limit on the authorisation of mergers is unworkable.

The Philip Morris decision

These and other disadvantages were referred to by the Commission in its 1966 Memorandum on Concentrations as reasons for not extending Article 85 to changes of ownership as such. However, none of these considerations deterred the European Court from ruling in *Philip Morris* in November 1987 that all agreements for merger where a cartel situation already existed or might be created by the merger were exposed to Article 85, rejecting the long held view that Article 85 did not apply to share transactions.

Philip Morris, one of six large groups dominating the cigarette market in the EC (described by the Court as stagnant and oligopolistic), agreed to acquire a 21.9 per cent shareholding in one of its competitors, Rothmans International, from its holding company, Rembrandt. The proposals had already been restructured after lengthy negotiations with the Commission to meet previous objections, and the Court held that the new arrangements did not infringe Articles 85 or 86. The Court nevertheless laid down the principle that there was no basic difference between an agreement to purchase shares in a competitor and other types of agreement. Article 85(1) might, therefore, be infringed if an acquisition was likely to result in a change in the *competitive behaviour* of the companies involved.

After *Philip Morris* the Commission lost no time in using the threat of interim measures to block anti-competitive mergers, and the potency of Article 85 as a defence to a consortium takeover bid has been demonstrated in the *Irish Distillers* and *GEC/Siemens/Plessey* cases, discussed below. The Commission's readiness to use interim measures greatly increases the scope and potential for controlling mergers under Article 85 and, as a result, poses a real threat to the takeover bidder whose timetable may be irreparably disrupted by a well-timed complaint to the Commission or application to the national court for an injunction while the complaint is being investigated.

Using Article 85 to repel boarders

Scope and development of Philip Morris

A merger may be caught by Article 85 if at least two competitors or potential competitors are involved and the market behaviour of one or more of those concerned in the merger is likely to be influenced so as to distort competition and have an appreciable effect on trade between the member states. When considering agreements between multinationals with worldwide interests, account can be taken of their relationships outside the EC so that an economically as well as legally correct assessment can be made.

The following are examples of merger situations which may now fall within Article 85:

Minority shareholdings

- Article 85 may apply to an acquisition of a minority shareholding in a competitor in any of the following situations:
  1. Where the acquisition, or the terms of the agreement, give the purchaser *de facto* control of the competitor's commercial conduct
  2. Where there is an agreement for future commercial co-operation
  3. Where there is no such agreement, but the result is to create a structure likely to be used for commercial co-operation – for example, if there are provisions for control or joint representation on the board of the company in which shares are acquired
  4. 'Creeping mergers' where the acquiring company has power, by means such as option or pre-emption rights, to reinforce its position by taking effective control of the competitor at a later stage

Acquisition leaving a minority shareholding with a competitor

- Such a case occurred immediately after *Philip Morris*. A French can maker, Sofreb, was owned as to 66.6 per cent by a French steel group (Sacilor) and as to 33.4 per cent by a West German subsidiary of the US-controlled giant, Continental Can. The French steel company was proposing to sell its 66.6 per cent shareholding to a major French can maker, Carnaud. The Commission took the view that two direct competitors owning the share capital of Sofreb was liable to lead to co-operation between them which would be incompatible with the competition rules. However, when Carnaud offered to buy the West German company's minority interest so as to acquire 100 per cent control, the Commission withdrew its objection because the risk of anti-competitive co-operation would be eliminated and the full takeover of Sofreb would have only marginally increased Carnaud's share of the Community market.

Consortium situations

- Cases where a consortium of companies bids for the shares in a competitor are vulnerable to Article 85 on grounds both of the auction ring effect this may have on the share price and of the cartel relationship existing, or to be established, between the consortium members after completion of the merger. Both situations were alleged by the Commission to exist in the *Irish Distillers* case, where the consortium companies had agreed to divide the brands of the target company between themselves after successful completion of the takeover.

This precedent was followed by Plessey, which lodged a complaint with the Commission against the public bid for it by Siemens and GEC. Plessey alleged that the consortium of Siemens and GEC infringed Article 85. The Commission has indicated that there was a *prima facie* case that the acquisition agreement fell under Article 85(1) because it involved proposals for the joint purchase by two competitors of another competitor, subsequent joint operation by the bidders of certain of Plessey's operations and co-operation between the bidders and their newly acquired joint venture. However, after a preliminary investigation the Commission announced its provisional conclusion that the EC competition rules would not be infringed, provided certain conditions were met.

100 per cent takeovers

• There is a difference of opinion as to whether Article 85 can apply to the acquisition of a 100 per cent shareholding in a competitor. For Article 85 to apply, it is necessary to show that competition will be restricted or distorted through an actual or likely change in the commercial behaviour of competitors who remain independent. The separate economic identity of the target company will be destroyed when the purchaser acquires it and the vendor and purchaser will not remain linked by a company structure likely to encourage co-operation.

The Commission's view is that Article 85 may apply to a 100 per cent acquisition if the market is one where competition will be substantially affected. It has already been shown that Article 85 may apply to such an acquisition where the bidders have formed themselves into a consortium; and, if a market is particularly sensitive, even an outright sale of a subsidiary by one competitor to another may influence the subsequent market behaviour of the vendor, the purchaser or both.

It is more difficult to imagine cases in which Article 85 could apply to a takeover bid for a publicly held company, assuming that no competitor was a substantial shareholder and that the bidder did not belong to a consortium.

Even in the case of a 100 per cent acquisition, therefore, the market situation and shareholding structure of the target company, the vendor and the purchaser should be carefully considered before a decision is made as to whether Article 85 is applicable and whether the agreement or offer should be notified.

Defensive stakes

- The Court indicated in *Philip Morris* that the taking of a purely defensive stake in a competitor does not automatically fall within Article 85, unless it is accompanied by arrangements for management participation or other forms of co-operation, even if the investing firm is given a right of veto over certain important decisions but without a decisive influence or control over its affairs. In such a case, the purpose and effect of taking the minority stake would normally be to prevent other competitors from gaining control and thus to allow a larger number of independent competitors to continue in business.

At first sight this would seem to be a helpful guideline to UK companies vulnerable to foreign predators and anxious to maintain a level playing-field, by strategies such as that, recently followed in the UK insurance industry, of companies taking reciprocal minority shareholdings for defensive purposes. However, caution is necessary. As already noted, the anti-competitive purpose and effect of any bid on the market for shares in a target company has to be considered quite separately from the effect on the relevant product market. It remains to be seen whether, on these grounds, the Commission will take the view that defensive practices such as that followed by UK insurance companies are anti-competitive in the context of the shares market, even though they do not affect competition in relation to any products or services.

This also raises the interesting question of whether the use by public companies in other member states of devices to block takeover bids, such as shares with limited voting rights, voting trusts and limited partnerships, could be attacked under Article 85, on the grounds that they distort the cross-border market in shares!

The Draft Merger Regulation

This section refers to the Commission's amended proposal for a Council Regulation on the control of concentrations between undertakings (November 1988), the latest available draft at the time of writing.

Is there a Community dimension?

The Draft Merger Regulation requires 'concentrations' which result in the acquisition of a direct or indirect controlling interest in all or

Thresholds

part of an undertaking and which exceeds stated size thresholds (Community dimension) to be notified to the Commission before they are put into effect. Both share and asset purchases are included. The thresholds are that the worldwide turnover of all the undertakings together must exceed 1,000 million ecu (roughly £650 million) and the Community-wide turnover of at least two must exceed 100 million ecu (roughly £65 million). However, even if these size criteria are met, the Draft Merger Regulation will not apply if each of the undertakings achieves more than three-quarters of its Community-wide turnover in the same member state. Proposals by the Commission to narrow the Regulation's scope by increasing the turnover thresholds and reducing the single member state proportion are currently under discussion.

'Turnover' means pre-tax turnover for all goods and services in the last financial year but excludes turnover from a group's internal operations. (The value of premiums received is substituted for turnover in the case of insurance companies, and one-tenth of the assets is substituted in the case of banking and financial institutions.)

Joint ventures aimed at, or resulting in co-ordination of the competitive behaviour of the parent company are outside the Draft Merger Regulation and are governed by Articles 85 or 86, but permanent and independent joint ventures without such anti-competitive implications do come within the Regulation. (It is not clear whether for this purpose a 'deadlock' joint venture company, under which no one group has control, would be covered by the Regulation.)

Is the merger compatible with the Common Market?

Every merger which comes within the scope of the Draft Merger Regulation as described above will be appraised by the Commission to determine whether it is compatible with the Common Market. It will be incompatible if it creates or strengthens a position as a result of which the maintenance or development of effective competition would be impeded in the Common Market or in a substantial part of it (the words 'dominant position' are avoided in the latest draft).

The Commission's appraisal must be made by reference to the market position and economic and financial power of the parties; to opportunities available to suppliers and users; to access to suppliers or markets; to the structure of the markets affected, taking account of international competition; to legal and factual barriers to entry; and to supply and demand trends for the relevant goods or services. The Commission may make its approval of a merger subject to specified conditions and obligations designed to safeguard effective competition.

Two points should be emphasised. First, it is the *result* of the creation or strengthening of a market position which is all important. It will not be enough for the Commission merely to show that the merger will create or strengthen such a market position if the maintenance or development of effective competition would not be likely to be impaired.

Second, the Commission must have regard to the future development of competition, not merely the position as it exists among the companies competing in the market at the date of the merger. To do this the Commission will, presumably, have regard to barriers to entry likely to deter new market entrants and to whether a result of the merger is likely to be a significant raising of those barriers.

Are there benefits to justify authorising an anti-competitive merger?

Where the Commission finds that a merger will create or strengthen a position as a result of which the maintenance or development of effective competition is impeded in the Common Market or a substantial part of it, it will have power, instead of declaring the merger incompatible with the Commn Market, to authorise it on a similar basis to exemptions granted under Article 85(3). The Commission must be satisfied that specific conditions are met – essentially, that the threatened damage to competition is outweighed by benefits in the form of improving production and distribution, promoting technical or economic progress or improving the competitive structure within the Common Market. An authorisation may cover reasonable ancillary restrictions in the merger arrangements.

What is the timetable?

Notification

The duty to notify an acquisition or takeover bid falls on the acquiring company and, in the case of mergers in the strict sense, on the parties jointly. A notification must be given immediate publicity in the Official Journal with the names of parties, nature of the merger and economic sectors involved. Business secrets (presumably including the offer price, where documents have not yet been sent out) are protected.

Proceedings

Within one month after the date of notification (which is not complete until all the necessary information has been supplied) the Commission must decide whether the proposed merger falls within the scope of the Draft Merger Regulation and, if so, must commence formal proceedings.

Having begun proceedings, the Commission must either, within one month, give clearance (with or without conditions attached) that the merger is compatible with the Common Market according to the criteria described above or, within four months, either declare the merger incompatible with the Common Market or authorise it on grounds of its compensating benefits.

Suspension   Pending the Commission's decision as to whether the merger comes within the scope of the Regulation, all action to carry out the merger must be suspended. The Commission may extend the period of suspension until a final decision is taken on the merger's compatibility with the Common Market.

The suspension during the first month and the possible extended period does not apply to a public takeover or exchange bid, provided this has been notified to the Commission at the same time as it is publicly announced. Such a bid may go ahead immediately, provided the voting rights attached to the shares are not exercised. All the suspension requirements and conditions may be waived by the Commission to prevent 'serious damage', with or without conditions.

How wide are the Commission's powers?

For those who comply with it, the Regulation is an improvement of the Article 86 regime. It provides criteria for notification, a workable timetable (which could however be improved by shortening the time limits) and a system for authorising beneficial mergers with anti-competitive features.

Conversely, the Commission is given wide powers to deal with those who fail to notify mergers or to provide information demanded of them. These include powers to order divestiture of unauthorised mergers and powers to carry out investigations and impose very large fines, subject to review by the European Court (which is given power to increase fines as well as to cancel or reduce them).

National and EC competition laws

Double jeopardy under Articles 85 and 86

Community law allows a merger to be subject to parallel proceedings and double sanctions under both national laws and Articles 85 and 86 but insists that, if there is a conflict, Community law must prevail. This rule was laid down in the European Court in 1969 when a West

German court sought guidance as to whether the German Federal Cartel Office could continue with national cartel proceedings when the same facts were being investigated by the Commission under Article 85.

National authorities may prohibit a merger on which the Commission has decided to take no action and may apply both national law and their own interpretation of Articles 85 and 86 in arriving at their decision. However, the national authority may not authorise a merger which the Commission has prohibited and arguably (although the point has yet to be decided by the European Court) it may not prohibit a merger which the Commission has exempted under Article 85(3), as opposed to one where it simply decided to take no action.

National merger policies

On pp. 166–82 we examine the interaction of EC and domestic competition laws in relation to an acquisition of a minority interest or majority stake in a local company in France, West Germany, Spain and Italy. Reference is also made to the table in Appendix I extracted from a CBI Working Paper, summarising general prohibitions, sectoral prohibitions and corporate shareholding and cultural factors affecting cross-border acquisitions of companies in the above member states and also in Belgium, the Netherlands and the UK.

The CBI table highlights the fact that local laws may apply to merger proposals not only on competition grounds but on other grounds, for example where it is deemed to be in the national interest to prevent foreign control in certain sectors such as maritime and air transport, banking and insurance. In the UK, a merger referred to the Monopolies and Mergers Commission (MMC) for investigation is appraised according to whether it may be expected to operate against the 'public interest'. In making such an appraisal the MMC is not limited to competition questions but is supposed to consider all factors which appear relevant: the balanced distribution of industry and employment in the UK is listed as relevant and, in the past, the MMC has also examined the effect on the balance of payments and on imports. The present Government's policy is to base its decisions solely on competition considerations unless there are very exceptional reasons to do otherwise.

Will the Merger Regulation prevent double jeopardy?

If adopted in its present form the Draft Merger Regulation will give the Commission sole competence to make decisions on mergers within the scope of the Regulation, whether or not the merger is adjudged to be compatible with the Common Market. National legislation on competition is excluded save that the Commission can, when approving a merger, attach conditions and authorise the member state concerned to apply national legislation to provide for effective competition in the local market.

There is also a saving clause to allow member states to apply measures, compatible with Community law, to protect their legitimate interests outside the sphere of competition, provided these interests are sufficiently defined and protected in the national law. It is impossible without litigation before the European Court to say which provisions of the type shown in the table on pp. 198–202 will pass the tests of sufficient definition and compatibility. Companies will no doubt play safe and notify their agreements to the national authorities where there is any room for doubt. It is uncertain whether the criterion of public interest under the 1973 Fair Trading Act, which is unlimited in its potential scope and embraces competition, will meet the test of sufficient definition.

Interface of the Draft Merger Regulation with Articles 85 and 86

The position where the Draft Merger Regulation does not apply

The Draft Merger Regulation is narrow in scope. Where it does not apply, the Commission and the national courts will be free to apply Articles 85 and 86 and national competition laws will have to be complied with. Exclusion from the Regulation will, therefore, expose the parties to a merger to fines, attack on the legal validity of the merger in the national courts and parallel national competition investigations. It is also likely to result in a spate of protective notifications.

Example

Megaton Enterprises Plc, with a worldwide turnover of £1,500 million, offers to acquire 100 per cent of Leviathan Plc, which belongs to a group with a turnover of £1,200 million. Both groups achieve 80 per cent of their EC turnover in the UK.

The merger is not notifiable under the Regulation. Instead, the Commission, or the national courts, may invoke Articles 85 and 86. Megaton may therefore decide to notify the merger to the Commission as well as to the Office of Fair Trading.

If either Megaton or Leviathan had only 70 per cent of their EC turnover in the UK, the Regulation would apply, Articles 85 and 86 would be excluded and notification to the Office of Fair Trading would be unnecessary unless directed by the Commission.

The Article 85 nightmare

At first sight, the Draft Merger Regulation appears to remove mergers which fall within its scope from exposure to Articles 85 and 86, at least so far as enforcement by the Commission is concerned. However, the present draft text appears to exclude from the Regulation all, or virtually all, cases where Article 85 would be capable of applying. It is stated that an operation with the object or effect of 'co-ordinating the competitive behaviour of two independent undertakings' is not to be treated as a 'concentration' to which the Regulation applies. These words are wide enough to cover virtually all merger situations which *Philip Morris* has brought within the ambit of Article 85.

The hapless business executive will thus be faced with the choice as to whether a merger which apparently meets all the criteria under the Regulation should be notified under it, or whether there is any possibility of the merger leading to a co-ordination of competitive behaviour which would make Article 85 apply instead. The spectre is **Double notifications** raised of having to make *double notifications* to protect the acquiring company against the consequences of making the wrong choice.

The Article 86 hangover

It is also unfortunate that Article 86 will continue to apply, under the *Continental Can* principle, to mergers which do not fall within the scope of the Regulation. The intention of the Regulation was to introduce a 'one-stop' merger control, described by Commissioner Sir Leon Brittan as 'a system whereby, in the case of smaller mergers, they would be subject only to national regulation . . . while in the case of the really large mergers which have implications for the whole Community, the European Commission would have the power to intervene, and companies would not normally need to be concerned about the national regulatory authorities'.

Double jeopardy This aim is not fulfilled where the parties are exposed to double jeopardy (attack by the Commission or in national courts under Article 86 on the *Continental Can* principle and also the operation of the relevant national competition laws) merely because the parties' turnover is below the Regulation's thresholds or because more than 75 per cent of the turnover of all parties is achieved in the same member state.

Some possible solutions

It is with some hesitation that we suggest possible solutions to the problems just outlined. By the time this book is in the reader's hands, the Council of Ministers may already have adopted the Draft Merger Regulation. There is, however, no sign that, when the Regulation is adopted, anything will have been done about the problem of its narrow scope and the continued operation of Articles 85 and 86 and national merger control rules outside its ambit. Therefore, whether the Regulation is adopted or not, business executives in a position to do so may wish to impress on their MEPs and Commission officials the urgency of finding comprehensive and workable solutions.

Short of amending the Treaty of Rome, nothing can be done about the continued direct effect of Articles 85 and 86 in the member states. But it would help the business community if the Commission were to recognise that share transactions have special requirements which call for a separate notification procedure. This could be achieved by drafting new regulations for notifying and scrutinising share transactions, on the following lines:

Notification procedures

- Time limits for clearance and authorisation to correspond to those in the Merger Regulation

- No requirement to fix a time limit for exemption under Article 85(3)

- A block exemption for two-party mergers and acquisitions, perhaps with an upper limit as to turnover thresholds, covering the agreements, warranties and indemnities, non-competition vendor convenants, pre-emption clauses and other matters commonly found in a straightforward acquisition or takeover bid

It would further simplify matters if the Merger Regulation were to state that mergers notified under it would automatically be treated as also notified under the new Article 85 procedure for share transactions suggested above.

In his address to the European Parliament in January 1988, Commissioner Peter Sutherland urged the adoption of the Merger Regulation to achieve 'clear, coherent, transparent and one-off decision making rather than the present situation which is totally antipathetic to developing a coherent strategy. Companies and individuals do not know where they are because of the different authorities in different member states and the added possibility that the Commission will come in on top of all of these authorities and come to a different conclusion. We want to avoid that.'

The reality of the proposal in its present form falls short of that aim. It is to be hoped that the Commission and the Council of Ministers will take action to narrow the gap.

10. Implementing the options

The Community options

It has not been the purpose of this book to turn business executives into lawyers, for that would improve neither the quality of their business decisions nor the reliability of their legal advice. Nor has it been the purpose of this book to give any credence to the belief that EC rules create complications for enterprises doing business across the national frontiers of the member states. On the contrary, we have tried to emphasise throughout that the Community system is designed to liberate business enterprise from the confines of individual national markets with differing legal requirements and to equip them for expansion in a single market comprising the territory of all the member states. In taking advantage of the opportunities afforded by the single market, we believe that legal input on the EC implications of a business strategy will become as routine a background to decision making as advice on the financial, commercial and technical implications of that strategy. For the new legal environment is an intrinsic part of the new commercial environment.

In order to make a success of competing in Europe it is necessary:

- To take advantage of EC rules allowing penetration of the European market

- To avoid violation of the Community rules by taking good advice and following it

- To be prepared to invoke the Community rules to ensure that competitors are themselves complying with their obligations

Corporate transactions across national frontiers

As the previous chapters have indicated, Community law enhances corporate commercial opportunities in the EC in a number of ways.

The provision of services – Community law provides for business transactions to be conducted across national frontiers

- Without it being essential to establish an agency, branch or subsidiary if this is not commercially attractive

- Without discrimination on grounds of nationality

- Subject to compliance only with those national legal provisions absolutely necessary to protect consumers and the public interest

Freedom of establishment – Community law entitles UK companies, if they so wish, to establish agencies, branches or subsidiaries in the territory of other member states without discrimination on grounds of nationality.

Company law harmonisation – Community law is providing increasingly for the simplification of national rules governing the licensing and conduct of various business activities, and in important sectors is placing the main burden of responsibility for authorising firms to conduct a particular business activity upon the member state where the head office of the firm in question is located ('home country control').

The EEIG and the European Company – In the near future, it will be possible for companies to establish new corporate forms based on Community law – the European Economic Interest Grouping, and perhaps the European Company. These possibilities will simplify transactions which are often at present complicated by the diverse and even conflicting requirements of national legal systems.

Implementing the options

Establishment and services

In order to take full advantage of the Community rules guaranteeing freedom of establishment and freedom to provide services, it may be necessary as a last resort for a company to assert its rights by legal process in national courts or by taking other appropriate enforcement action. The provisions of the Treaty of Rome guaranteeing the right of establishment and the right to provide services across national frontiers are directly enforceable in the courts of all the member states against public authorities and against other companies which impede the full exercise of these rights. Appropriate provisions of Directives may be enforced against public authorities, though not against individuals or companies. Directives play an important role in all member states in the interpretation of the national laws adopted to secure their implementation.

From the legal point of view, getting established in another market will mean considering the options Community law provides against the relevant commercial and legal background of the potential host state. If setting up a subsidiary is involved, or entering into a distributorship with a local undertaking, this will require advice from the firm of solicitors which advises on the European aspects of your affairs. Increasingly they will have links with colleagues in other member states. They will also advise you that Community law takes precedence over national law, and that apparent legal obstacles in a potential neighbouring market may sometimes be overcome without undue friction.

Sometimes, friction may be unavoidable. For example, suppose that the authorities of a member state refused to recognise the right of a UK company to undertake certain business in its territory because of the existence of discriminatory national requirements, and threatened prosecution. Suppose further that a client in the state in question thereupon refused to pay money due under contracts with the UK company on the ground that the contracts were illegal and unenforceable because the UK company was infringing the requirements of local law. If the company's lawyer advised that the company was entitled under Community law to do business in that state, and negotiations failed, the company might have no choice but to defend and/or initiate legal proceedings before the national courts in that state. These courts might make a reference to the European Court and, if the case were taken to a level from which there was no appeal, a reference to the European Court would be obligatory. Such legal proceedings at the national level might be backed up by a complaint to the Commission, which has a general responsibility for enforcing the provisions of Community law. If necessary, the Commission might itself initiate an investigation of the conduct of the member state in question, and even open proceedings against that state before the European Court. A sympathetic MEP might put a question to the Commission on the predicament of the company in question and the conduct of the national authorities. The very fact of a complaint having been made to the Commission might create a climate in the national proceedings which could make reference to the European Court more likely.

Market dominance

Competition policy

Protection from unfair competition – The purpose of the EC competition rules is to ensure that cartels and dominant enterprises do not inhibit the establishment and functioning of the single market. Legal protection against unfair competition and anti-competitive practices may require initiating legal proceedings before UK courts, or simply a complaint backed by argument and evidence to the Commission, which will then take the appropriate action; this can include opening an investigation which culminates in a fine. It has been demonstrated that a small or medium-sized enterprise penetrating a new market may find the enforcement of the EC competition rules by national courts and by the Commission crucial to its commercial future. There may again be cases where a company feels aggrieved because a competitor has been the beneficiary of an exemption which the company is advised is unjustified. It may be open to the company to challenge that exemption before the European Court. Furthermore, recourse to the Commission can provide protection against the dumping of products from countries outside the Community at unfairly low prices – the Commission may impose provisional duties to offset this unfair competitive advantage and these duties may be made definitive by the Council.

Competition law: the duty to comply – In developing business strategies appropriate to a single market embracing the territory of twelve countries, tailoring commercial transactions to market realities means tailoring them to the legal realities of the Community competition rules. The substance and procedure of these rules have been outlined in the foregoing chapters. To avoid infringing the EC competition rules, it is necessary to take good legal advice at the planning stage, rather than waiting for the Commission or a competitor to take legal action. Working relationships should be struck up between in-house lawyers and outside specialist advisers and, where appropriate, Commission personnel. If a single point is to be emphasised to companies seeking to avoid conflict with the requirements of the competition rules, it is the wisdom of adopting a compliance programme, whereby those areas of commercial activity most likely to be affected by the rules are indentified in advance, relevant personnel are given appropriate instruction in company policy, and relevant documents are retained by the company in order to safeguard its position should a Commission investigation or other proceedings materialise.

Marketing strategy and licensing – The marketing of products in different member states may be facilitated by recourse to:

- Exclusive distribution

- Selective distribution

- Franchising

- Licensing

- Sales agencies

While all the above arrangements have features which may restrict competition and inter-state trade, they are also recognised as making a positive contribution to competition in the Common Market, provided that their terms comply with the requirements of the Community competition rules. Where advice is taken on the scope of applicable block exemptions, and notification is made to the Commission in appropriate cases, the above marketing matters constitute invaluable options in the single market.

Joint ventures – Small and medium-sized businesses may find that mutual co-operation provides the basis for commercial expansion in the Common Market, and the establishment of a joint subsidiary or other business entity may provide an ideal vehicle for collaboration. Where competitors or potential competitors are involved, the competition rules may apply, but the Commission has stressed that certain kinds of co-operation, in particular those involving joint research and development and specialisation between the participating enterprises, are capable of improving the climate of competition in the Community and benefiting consumers. Such agreements are eligible for exemption by the Commission, and even joint ventures involving large enterprises have been granted exemption. Other types of joint venture, in particular joint sales arrangements, restrict competition between participating enterprises without compensating benefits, and accordingly cannot qualify for exemption. The exchange of confidential business information likely to influence the market behaviour of competitors may infringe the competition rules.

Mergers and takeovers – Mergers and takeovers may provide a means whereby companies adjust their activities to the scale of the single market. At the present stage of Community law, national competition and stock exchange rules co-exist with the application of the Community competition rules. It is clear that a takeover by a firm in a dominant position of an actual or potential competitor may amount to an abuse of a dominant position. It now seems that the rules prohibiting restrictive trading arrangements may apply to the agreements whereby a merger or takeover is accomplished. As we explain in Chapter 9 there is in addition a Proposal for a Regulation which would expressly subject certain mergers and acquisitions with a Community dimension to Commission scrutiny currently pending before the Council.

Conclusion

In the Commission's publication *Developing an Active Company Approach to the European Market*, businesses are reminded of the importance of EC law in the completion of the internal market:

> It is not just the abolition of frontiers and the opportunities to provide goods and services to 320 million consumers which is at stake. Perhaps more important is that legislation on standards, freedom of establishment, trademarks and patents, company law . . . to mention but a few, will enable efficient companies to sell and compete more effectively, even in their home markets.

As was noted at the beginning of this chapter, it is no part of the purpose of this book to turn business executives into lawyers. However, business executives and lawyers need to work together to develop the Community reflex – the instinct that reminds where there is a Community aspect to a problem and indicates an appropriate Community solution. The authors hope that our book will make a useful contribution to this process and so help to make 1992 a reality.

III
Case notes and studies

Towards a single market in insurance: a success story

Background: The obstacles to a single market

Historically, an insurance company in one member state seeking to penetrate the markets of the others faced a daunting task. The obstacles were of two kinds.

Firstly, strict regulations, designed to protect the interests of insured persons, were different in each member state. These rules frequently discriminated against companies incorporated in other member states, either in their express terms or through the way they operated in practice. Thus, a company wishing to establish itself in another member state would have to comply simultaneously with more than one regulatory system.

Secondly, the provision of services on an occasional basis from an office in one member state to a customer in another was effectively ruled out by the provisions of national law in the latter state.

The Treaty prohibited discrimination. It was recognised at an early stage of the development of the Common Market that the insurance sector was 'a suitable case for treatment', in terms of establishing a true single market. The appropriate treatment was to consist of legislation at the Community level, coupled with rulings of the European Court, at the instigation of the Commission, insisting on the member states giving full and proper effect to the requirements of the Treaty.

The technique employed was to co-ordinate and strengthen the national rules for protection of insured persons by introducing clear rules

- To allocate responsibility to national authorities for the authorisation of insurance companies and supervision of their activities

- To provide, in place of isolated national regulatory systems, a mixture of common standards to be applied throughout the Community or, as an alternative, mutual recognition of national regulations in those areas where standardisation was not essential

The Community's progress towards a single market in the insurance sector has taken place over twenty-five years and has accelerated with the drive to achieve the single internal market by the end of 1992. We outline below the stages by which progress has been achieved.

Removal of national restrictions: re-insurance

The first step towards removing national restrictions was taken by a Directive adopted in 1964, relating to re-insurance. This Directive prohibited discriminatory requirements for re-insurers under the laws of West Germany, France, Belgium, Luxembourg and Italy, requiring special authorisations from companies from other member states wishing to provide re-insurance services in those countries.

The Directive did no more than reiterate the prohibition on discrimination contained in the Treaty of Rome. At the time, it was not appreciated that the Treaty could itself be invoked in litigation before the national courts.

The right to establish branches and agencies: the First Non-life Insurance Directive

An important step was taken in July 1973 when the Community issued a Directive to harmonise the laws of the member states relating to the establishment of agencies and branches of insurance companies offering direct insurance, including for example accident and sickness insurance and commercial insurance (such as ships and aircraft). Life insurance was excluded, but was later covered by a Directive in substantially similar terms in 1979.

The 1973 Directive was designed to co-ordinate rules and practices for the supervision of insurers and, particularly, of their financial stability. Responsibility was allocated for supervising insurance **Head Office/** undertakings between, on the one hand, the member state where the **Host State** head office was situated ('the Head Office State') and, on the other hand, the member state where an agency or branch of a company with a head office in another member state was carrying on business ('the Host State').

All member states were obliged to make the taking up of insurance business in their territory subject to the issue of an official authorisation. The Head Office State was required to prescribe an adequate solvency margin, calculated under rules laid down in the Directive, for the entire business of insurance companies with their head offices in its territory, and to verify that the state of solvency of those companies adhered to the prescribed margins. The authorities of Host States were required to provide the Head Office State with all necessary information for this purpose.

Each Head Office State was directed to require insurance companies with head offices in its territory to provide annual accounts covering all their activities, their financial situation and their solvency. In contrast, each Host State was given the responsibility of requiring the company to establish sufficient technical reserves in accordance with the rules applied in that state.

Both the Head Office State and the Host State were empowered to withdraw authorisation from insurance companies no longer fulfilling the prescribed requirements. However, the Host State was required to consult the Head Office State before doing so, unless the situation called for immediate action, in which case the Host State was required to advise the Head Office State immediately of the action taken.

Opening the way for cross-border insurance services

The rules so far described are confined to establishing agencies or branches in a member state by insurance companies with a head office in another member state. They do not deal with a situation in which a company established in one state provides services in another, i.e. insures risks in another member state without having an agency, branch or establishment there.

Two developments in recent years have made it possible to tackle the main outstanding barriers. First, in four key insurance cases decided by the European Court in 1986 concerning insurance regulations in West Germany, France, Denmark and the Republic of Ireland, the Court laid down valuable guidelines on conducting business on a services basis in the insurance sector. Secondly, the extension into the insurance field of qualified majority voting by the Single European Act as from 1 July 1987 removed the ability of individual member states to block proposals in isolation.

The European Court's guidelines

In the 1986 rulings referred to above, the European Court demonstrated that Community legislation is not the only means for removing barriers to the internal market. Member states can be required, purely on the basis of the Treaty itself, to abolish restrictive regulations and practices, without the need to await the adoption of Directives or to implement national legislation.

The Commission's enforcement action against West Germany was provoked by the German Insurance Supervision Law. This included provisions that:

- Foreign insurance companies wishing to carry out direct insurance operations in West Germany through salesmen, agents, etc. must be authorised by the West German authorities

- Such companies must set up 'an establishment' in West Germany and 'keep available there all the commercial documents relating to that establishment', for which separate accounts must also be kept

- For certain categories of insurance, although there was no requirement of establishment, there was a requirement for undertakings to be authorised

The Court held that West Germany could not make it a condition of providing insurance services that a company established in another member state must open an agency or branch in West Germany. The Treaty guaranteed the freedom of the company to carry on business through mail order, agents or sales representatives. Furthermore, in the Court's view, in certain fields of insurance the Community rules provided substantially equivalent conditions for doing business in the various member states and in those fields it was no longer permissible for West Germany to require that a company established in another member state must submit to West German authorisation procedures.

More generally, the Court ruled that unduly restrictive and unnecessary rules could not be applied to companies providing insurance services without a place of business in West Germany. The Court clearly thought that it would be unduly restrictive to require authorisation for insurance services provided by out-of-state insurance companies for commercial customers in West Germany, since such customers are capable of safeguarding their own interests.

Developments following the European Court's judgments

Following the Court's 1986 judgments the way was opened for the Commission to press ahead with new proposals to create a single EC insurance market.

Credit, suretyship and legal expenses

In 1987, Directives were adopted for credit and suretyship insurance and legal expenses insurance which, as well as laying down additional financial and other requirements for such insurance, brought to an end West Germany's specialisation requirements for these classes of insurance.

In June 1988 the important Non-life Insurance Services Directive was adopted. This lays down rules, conceptually based on the 1986 judgments, under which cross-border non-life insurance business (excluding motor liability insurance) may be carried out on a services basis.

Large risks and mass risks

The Directive regulates two different types of risk. A simplified regime applies where the insurer wishes to cover only 'large risks' – industrial and commercial risks defined in the regulation and including all marine, aviation and transport business. In other cases ('mass risks'), the authorities in the state where the risk is located will still be able to impose an authorisation requirement and to supervise scales of premiums, policy conditions and the reserves held to meet underwriting liabilities.

An insurer established within the Community which wishes to supply only 'large risk' insurance services in another member state only has to comply with the notification procedure of the Directive. This requires the insurer to produce certificates issued by the authorities of its Head Office State, firstly, stating that it possesses for its activities as a whole the minimum solvency margin prescribed under the 1973 Directive and that it is authorised to operate outside the Head Office State; and, secondly, indicating the classes of insurance which the insurer is authorised to cover and declaring that the Head Office State authorities do not object to the insurer providing services. The insurer must also state the nature of the risks proposed to be covered in the Host State.

For 'mass risks' the procedure for authorisation may take longer. The Host State may require a 'scheme of operations' to be submitted where, in addition to the particulars required for 'large risks', details must be given of the proposed policy conditions, premium rates and (so far as these are required from other insurance companies in the Host State) the forms and other printed documents which it is intended to use.

The insurer may have to wait up to six months for authorisation from the Host State authorities, although some of the detailed requirements listed in the Directive for obtaining authorisation are discretionary.

The difference of regime applicable to 'large' and 'mass' risks also extends to the regulation of technical reserves. For 'large risks', technical reserves must be constituted in accordance with the law of the Head Office State and be supervised by the authorities of that state. For 'mass risks', technical reserves must be constituted in accordance with the law (or established practice) of the Host State and supervised by the authorities of the Host State.

Following the adoption of the Non-life Insurance Services Directive the Commission has now adopted a Proposal for a Directive to co-ordinate national laws to provide services in the area of life assurance. The Proposal distinguishes between where an insurer actively canvasses for customers in another member state without having to create an establishment in that other state and the situation where the prospective policy holder upon his own initiative seeks life assurance in another member state whether by telephone, letter or through a broker. In the first case where the insurer takes the initiative, the host country can require the insurer to seek authorisation which may depend on domestic rules on technical reserves and conditions of insurance. However, where the prospective policy holder takes the initiative the supervisory rules of the home country will apply.

Pensions and other collective life assurance business and individual contracts relating to the insured's employment are excluded from the current proposal but the matter is currently undergoing discussions which may result in coverage extending to some aspects of business related policies.

Further proposals are also under consideration by the Commission at the present time for harmonisation of the rules regarding the annual accounts and the winding up of insurance companies and for the co-ordination of rules relating to insurance contracts.

The future

To sum up, the procedures provided for in the Treaty of Rome for harmonising national rules and enforcing the implementation of those rules by judicial action if necessary, have gone a long way towards creating a single market in insurance. The process is not yet complete, and is continuing. It must be noted that insurance undertakings themselves are entitled to assert their rights under Community law before national courts, should the need arise.

One fact is incontestable. UK insurance companies will enjoy greater opportunities to provide insurance services in other member states in the 1990s than they enjoyed in the 1970s or even the 1980s. The EC has the second largest insurance market after the USA. The UK is in the top five national markets of the EC. One of the strengths of the UK insurance market has been its success in selling to foreign policy-holders. The UK insurer will be likely, therefore, to derive benefit from a single market in insurance services. Access by foreign insurers to the UK insurance market will not be radically altered, since the UK has never restricted foreign insurers unlike many other member states have done in the past.

The *Hudson's Bay* case

This case study is based on the Commission decision reported in the Official Journal of 23 November 1988 (OJ 1988 L316/43). It is a good example of how a company can seek the protection of the Commission from unfair competitive practices, as discussed in Chapter 5.* It also illustrates how private business practices would be quite capable in certain economic sectors of partitioning a national market from the other national markets in the absence of the EC competition rules. These rules thus constitute an essential supplement to the Treaty of Rome provisions which prohibit governmental measures such as customs duties and quotas, which have in the past partitioned the national markets. The agreements in issue, which were held to infringe the EC competition rules, were not notified until after the investigation was initiated (and then only in part), and therefore a fine could be imposed.

Origin of the complaint

Hudson's Bay and Annings Ltd, London (HBA), the principal auctioneer of furs in the UK, acquired furs from Denmark through the agency of certain traders in Denmark. These latter traders were members of the Danish Fur Breeders' Association (DPF). Disciplinary action by the DPF against these members for acting for HBA led to the investigation in question.

The Danish Fur Breeders' Association

The DPF is a co-operative association comprising over 5,000 fur breeders (the furs in question being mink, fox, racoon and fitch). It provides for its members an advisory and consultancy service, educational facilities, a monthly magazine and experimental and

* S J Berwin & Co acted in this case for Hudson's Bay and Annings Ltd, the complainant.

research operations. Certain services are free to members, others must be paid for. The DPA is the selling branch of the DPF and conducts fur auctions.

The rules of the DPF obliged members not to organise or support sales by competitors of the DPF. These rules were invoked against two undertakings which had acted for HBA in Denmark, and these undertakings were expelled from the DPF. These expulsions caused great hardship to the traders concerned, since they were dependent as fur breeders upon a number of the services provided by the DPF, and those services were not available elsewhere. HBA took legal advice with a view to safeguarding the rights of the expelled traders and were advised of the possibility that the rules of the DPF might infringe the EC competition rules.

Collecting the evidence

The fur breeder members of the DPF were reluctant to give evidence against their own trade associations for fear of recriminations, yet some were willing to give evidence to solicitors for HBA on the basis that statements would be treated in confidence by the Commission.

The Commission carried out on-the-spot investigations in Copenhagen and, exercising their powers under Community law, required the DPA to provide further information.

Rules and practices of the Association

In addition to requiring members not to organise or support sales by competitors of the DPA, the rules and practices of the DPA:

- Made the grant of emergency assistance conditional upon a member supplying for sale only the DPA

- Made certain financial advantages conditional upon the member supplying for sale only the DPA

- Made inclusion in a list of breeders producing quality furs conditional upon the member consigning his entire farm production for sale by the DPA

Furthermore, the DPA operated a quota system whereby a percentage of each member's production was sold at each of the DPA's auctions held annually.

Complaint, investigation and notification

The complaint of HBA was submitted on 4 January 1985. At that time no notification of the rules applied by the DPF had been made to the Commission. During the course of the Commission's investigation, on 27 August 1985, the DPF notified certain rules and decisions to the Commission, no doubt with a view to protecting themselves against fines in the future. This notification, however, could not safeguard the DPF from fines with respect to periods prior to notification, and in fact a substantial fine was imposed (see below).

Commission finds infringement of Article 85(1)

The Commission found that the rules that applied between the DPF and its members were agreements between undertakings (the fur breeders) which restricted competition and affected inter-state trade. The rules included among their objects the prevention of the consignment or sale of furs by DPF members to any of DPF's competitors by obliging the DPF members to sell 100 per cent of their production through the DPA. Trade between member states was affected since it was the aim of the rules in question to limit market entry by competitors by virtually monopolising the supply and sale of mink skins in Denmark. Limiting or eliminating effective competition had resulted in partitioning the Common Market in as much as Denmark was virtually inaccessible to competitors of the DPF. The Commission took the view that if the 100 per cent obligations were abolished or reduced a larger percentage of furs (especially mink) would be sent by DPF members to competitors of DPF including HBA, as in the case of the other Scandinavian countries. Members of the DPF were and had been prevented by the rules from sending part of their production to other member states either to be auctioned or as direct sales. Furthermore, as the possibility of Danish breeders selling privately to buyers in other member states was almost entirely eliminated (over 27 per cent of world mink production) the effects on trade between member states was appreciable.

Commission refuses exemption

The Commission refused exemption to the rules as they stood since their effect was to eliminate competition in respect of a substantial part of the products in question. Furthermore, it had not been established that the obligations in question were indispensable to achieving the objectives of the DPF.

No exemption or clearance for proposed changes

The Commission refused to consider the question of negative clearance or exemption for certain changes in the rules proposed by the DPF until those changes had actually been implemented.

Fines – aggravation and mitigation

The Commission imposed fines of 500,000 ecu. It has been noted above that notification of certain rules and decisions was only made after commencement of the investigation and that fines could thus be imposed for periods prior to notification even with respect to the rules and decisions notified.

The Commission believed that a fine was merited because the infringements were committed deliberately or at least negligently. The DPF must, in their view, have know that the 100 per cent obligations regarding sale through the DPA had as their object or effect the restriction of competition.

The infringements were regarded as serious by the Commission because they resulted in other fur trading agencies being almost totally excluded from obtaining supplies in Denmark and thus almost eliminated any competition with the DPF there.

Mitigating factors taken into account by the Commission were that during the investigation the DPF had made concrete proposals to eliminate the restrictions complained of, and the fact that DPF was a co-operative association deserved special consideration. A characteristic of co-operatives is that they are owned by farmers who in terms of their income depend directly on the business results of the co-operative.

The expelled members

As well as being fined and required to terminate all infringements, the DPF was required to inform the members which had been expelled because they had acted as agents for HBA that the obligation which led to their expulsion had been found to have infringed Article 85(1) of the Treaty of Rome. The DPF was required to forward to the Commission a copy of this communication and any replies thereto.

Sequel – anti-competitive merger prohibited by the Commission

All the Scandinavian Fur Breeders' Associations (i.e. Sweden, Finland, Denmark and Norway) were linked together through a local Scandinavian association of fur breeders' associations. A sequel to the above complaint was that the Finnish Fur Breeders' Association acquired HBA and endeavoured to sell a 35 per cent shareholding of HBA's share capital to the Danish association. The Norwegian association was to acquire a further 10 per cent and the Swedish association a further 5 per cent. At the time of announcing the proposed deal, reference was then made to the fact that detailed plans would be worked out covering HBA's position within the Scandinavian association. This was objected to by the Commission on the basis of the ruling in the *Philip Morris* case that an agreement between undertakings resulting in a change in the legal or factual control of another undertaking could be caught by Article 85 of the Treaty of Rome – in this case, the result of the sale of the shares would have been for the Danish association to determine the future conduct of its principal competitor in the EC, thereby reducing or eliminating competition. The Commission intervened of its own initiative, thereby illustrating that even in the absence of a complaint by an interested third party, the Commission will intervene in the public interest in appropriate cases. This is a further striking example of the flexibility and effectiveness of the interim measures procedure in the hands of the Commission.

The protection of commercial agents and distributors*

Snugfit Plc, a UK shoe manufacturer, sells its products in the EC through sole agents, all of whom are individuals, in France, West Germany and Italy and through a company which is an independent distributor in Belgium. All the agreements state that they can be terminated by three months' notice on either side and all have in fact been in operation for more than ten years.

The contracts for Belgium and West Germany state that English law applies, but is silent as to courts where disputes are to be determined. Those for France and Italy are subject to local law.

Snugfit proposes to terminate its current agreements and to set up a network of franchised outlets in each country. Can it do so, and at what cost?

Belgium

Belgian law is unlike that of other European countries, in that it gives special favourable treatment to distributors and to employed sales representatives, but has no special provisions for the protection of commercial agents. A commercial agency agreement can, therefore, be terminated unilaterally without notice or special indemnity, although unreasonable termination of the contract may give rise to a claim for damages.

The position of distributors is governed by the 'Law on the Unilateral Termination of Sales Concessions' dated 27 July 1961, as amended by a law of 13 April 1971. The Law is 'imperative' for agreements to which it applies, i.e. it can, in principle, be invoked by the distributor notwithstanding anything to the contrary in the agreement. The Law gives jurisdiction to the Belgian courts to hear any

---

* The following law firms have assisted S J Berwin & Co in the preparation of this case study: Rycken Burlion Bolle & Houben (Belgium); Gide Loyrette Nouel (France); Modest Gundisch Landry (West Germany); Studio Legale Bisconti (Italy).

litigation regarding the termination of a distributorship having its effect in all or part of the Belgian territory. Furthermore, the Belgian courts are directed to apply only Belgian law and to disregard any term of the contract that foreign law is to apply.

If, however, the agreement provides that sole jurisdiction relating to questions concerning the agreement is assigned to the courts of a country (other than Belgium) which has a real connection with the contract and is a signatory to the Treaty of Brussels of 1968 relating to jurisdiction and enforcement of judgments, Belgian law will not apply. The UK is a signatory to the Treaty and, therefore, had the agreement contained a clause providing that disputes would be determined by the English courts, as well as a requirement that the contract should be governed by English law, Belgian law would have been inapplicable. However, in the present case, Snugfit's agreement states only that English law will apply and is silent as to jurisdiction so that Belgian law has not been effectively excluded.

The main features of the Belgian statute are as follows:

- The Law applies to distributorships which are exclusive (or nearly so) and also, those where 'important obligations' are placed on the distributor, which would cause him to suffer serious harm if the contract were to be terminated.

- There are provisions for minimum notice periods and for compensation. However, these apply only where the contract is of 'indefinite duration', rather than for a fixed period. Note, however, that if a contract is renewed more than twice, it is treated as being for an indefinite period and, therefore, subject to the minimum notice and compensation provisions.

- If one party wishes to cancel the contract and is not entitled to do so on grounds of the other party's serious breach, the first party is given the option either of giving the other party 'reasonable notice', or of paying it a 'fair indemnity'. The length of the notice period and the amount of the termination indemnity may be determined by the parties only at the time when the notice of termination is given.

  The notice period must be long enough to permit the other party to find a distributorship for other products on favourable terms. If the parties fail to agree on a mutually acceptable notice period, the matter is determined by the courts, taking criteria fixed by case law into consideration, such as the length of the distributorship, the nature of its products and the importance to the distributor of continuing the distributorship. If the notice period is deemed not to be sufficient, the court determines the amount of the termination indemnity, taking into account profits which the distributor would have earned had a reasonable notice period been given.

- If a distribution agreement subject to the Law is terminated by the principal for reasons other than serious fault on the part of the distributor or if the distributor terminates because of serious fault on the part of the principal, the distributor can, in addition, claim a special indemnity, established on the facts of each case according to the following criteria: additional clientele which the principal has acquired as a result of the distributor's efforts; expenses incurred by the distributor which will benefit the principal after termination of the contract; and amounts which the distributor must pay to staff whom it is obliged to release as a result of the termination of the contract.

To sum up, therefore, Snugfit may have to pay the Belgian distributor a 'fair indemnity' if the three month notice period is not long enough to be considered as 'reasonable'. Snugfit will, in addition, be liable to pay a special indemnity for the benefit of additional clientele, expenses and redundancy payments as described above. The process of arriving at these figures is not clearly defined but, bearing in mind the length of time the distributorship has been in operation, compensation may prove expensive.

Snugfit could have avoided this liability by assigning jurisdiction to the English courts as well as providing that English law would apply; by entering into a distributorship agreement for a fixed term rather than an indefinite term (provided that this fixed term had not been renewed twice); or by appointing a commercial agent rather than a distributor in Belgium.

France

The position of commercial agents is governed by a Decree 58/1345 dated 23 December 1958, amended by a Decree 68/765 of 22 August 1968. This Decree provides that:

- The termination of the commercial agent's agreement by the principal, if not justified by fault on the part of the agent, confers on the agent a right to compensation for the losses suffered by him, notwithstanding any clause in the agreement to the contrary

- Refusal by the principal to renew an agreement whose fixed term has expired, does not give rise to such a right of compensation ('indemnity') unless the refusal is found to be 'abusive', i.e. motivated by an intention to damage the agent, or resulting from gross negligence

The method of determining the indemnity and its amount depends on the facts of the particular case. There are cases in which an agent has received an indemnity of as much as three years' commission for an unjustified termination by his principal.

The right to indemnity does not ordinarily arise in the case of an independent distributor. However, the courts have awarded indemnities to independent distributors in cases where the termination has been 'abusive'.

The Decree provides that a commercial agent must be registered with the Commercial Court and this is sanctioned by a fine. The above summary assumes that Snugfit's agent was so registered. However, many commercial agents carry on business without being registered and apparently with impunity. According to French case law, registration is a pre-requisite for commercial agent status and for the rights of compensation referred to above. Also, an agreement with a 'non-statutory agent' can be made subject to the law, and to the jurisdiction of the courts of the principal's country, if this is desired.

Snugfit could, therefore, have avoided liability by requiring the agent to be a 'non-statutory agent' (i.e. not to register himself with the Commercial Court) and the contract could then also have made the agreement subject to English law and to the jurisdiction of the English courts.

West Germany

The position of the commercial agent and the independent distributor is governed by the Commercial Code. Although distributors are not covered by the law which protects commercial agents, the courts have held that where the distributor's contract comes to an end, he is entitled to a compensation 'adjustment' claim just like a commercial agent.

The position of the commercial agent is governed by Section 84–92(c) of the Commercial Code. These provisions include an 'adjustment payment' as compensation for loss of commission and as consideration for the agent's efforts to enhance the principal's business and goodwill, the maximum being one year's commission averaged over the past five years (or the period of the agency, if shorter). There are also provisions governing the validity of restrictions on the activities of the commercial agent after termination of the agency.

All these provisions, however, can be excluded if the contract provides that another system of law is to apply. The West German Supreme Court has ruled that a contract whereby a foreign principal and a West German agent agreed that their relationship should be governed by the laws, and cases of dispute decided by the courts of the country in which the principal was a national and/or resident, was not contrary to the law of West Germany. There is also a specific ruling of the West German Supreme Court that the compensation provisions do not apply if the contract is governed by a foreign law which does not make provision for such compensation.

Therefore, Snugfit will have succeeded in escaping the compensation provisions through the provision in its contract with the West German agent applying English law.

Italy

Commercial agents are covered by articles 1742 to 1753 of the Italian Civil Code and by 'National Economical Agreements', which were given the force of law by presidential decrees in the years 1960 to 1961.

There does not appear to be any reason why the parties should not exclude the provisions of the Italian Civil Code by agreement, or to provide that a foreign system of law will apply to the agency agreement. Local custom is given considerable importance under the terms of the Code.

Article 1751 provides as follows regarding indemnity on the dissolution of an agency agreement for an indefinite period:

> If a contract for an indefinite period is dissolved for reasons which are not imputable to the agent, the principal is required to pay the agent an indemnity in proportion to the amount of commission received by the agent during the course of the contract and at the rate laid down by local custom or, in the absence of such custom, by the courts. From this indemnity would be deducted whatever the agent has received by way of voluntary social welfare payments paid by the principal. The indemnity is also payable even if the agency arrangement is dissolved as a result of the permanent and total physical incapacity of the agent. In the event of the agent's death, the indemnity is payable to the heirs.

Article 1743 of the Italian Civil Code provides that:

> The principal cannot avail himself simultaneously of several agents in the same area and for the same business, nor can the agent assume the task of handling in the same area and for the same product the business of several firms which are competing with each other.

Snugfit will accordingly find itself liable to pay an indemnity under Article 1751, determined according to the law and any applicable collective bargaining agreements. The amount of the indemnity is not limited save for the deduction of voluntary social welfare payments. These are likely to be substantial. A foreign principal who does not have a place of business or address in Italy, may, and generally will enrol its Italian agent with ENASARCO, a public agency charged with the administration of social security benefits for agents. As a condition for enrolment, the principal must sign a statement in which he agrees to abide by the provisions regulating ENASARCO enrolment and contributions, as well as applicable collective agreements.

Social security contributions amount to 10 per cent (5 per cent for the principal and 5 per cent for the agent) on all commissions or on other amounts, e.g. reimbursement for expenses, due to the agent in respect of agency relationship, up to a ceiling of 24 million lire per year for an exclusive agent and 10 million lire for a non-exclusive agent.

Italian law does not have any special provisions regarding distribution agreements (i.e. exclusive sales concession agreements). It is, however, probable that on a claim for compensation for termination of such an agreement, the Italian courts would apply by analogy the indemnity provisions relating to agency agreement.

Effect of the 1986 EC Directive

The Directive, 'On the coordination of the laws of the member states relating to self-employed commercial agents', required all the member states to change their domestic laws relating to self-employed commercial agents so as to comply with its provisions by not later than 1 January 1990. This date is extended until 1994 for the Republic of Ireland and the UK and (for the compensation provisions only) to 1993 for Italy. Agreements already in existence when the new legislation comes into force will have to be made subject to the new rules not later than 1 January 1994.

To date, of the countries dealt with in this case study only West Germany has so far tabled a law to implement the Directive. This received its first reading in September 1988 and the law is expected to be passed in 1989 and to come into force on 1 January 1990.

After the Directive has been implemented in the UK, and agreements become subject to the new provisions, there will cease to be any advantage in providing for English law to apply and for the English courts to have jurisdiction in disputes with commercial agents in other EC countries, although such a clause may still prove beneficial in agreements with distributors or with agents who are not brought within the ambit of the new legislation. Local legal advice should always be obtained before entering into an agency or distribution agreement.

Irish Distillers
Interaction between Articles 85 and 86 and domestic legislation

There is no better recent example of the practical interaction of merger control at a Community and national level than the *Irish Distillers* case.* The case study below discusses the history of the merger and traces its development and conclusion.

On 26 May 1988 Grand Metropolitan PLC and Allied Lyons PLC decided that their Irish subsidiaries, Gilbeys of Ireland Limited and Cantrell & Cochrane Limited, would jointly establish a new company called G C & C Brands Limited in which the shares would be held 50 per cent by Cantrell & Cochrane and 50 per cent by Gilbeys. Guinness PLC, which, through its Irish subsidiary, had a 49.6 per cent share of Cantrell & Cochrane, agreed to increase its holding in that company in order to enable it to join forces with Gilbeys in making a joint bid for Irish Distillers Group (IDG). Shortly afterwards G C & C Brands, by a decision of its board of directors, decided to bid for the entire ordinary share capital of IDG and offered 315 pence in cash per share. On 30 May 1988 the offer was made by G C & C at which time G C & C also announced that it held irrevocable acceptances from FII Fyffes PLC in respect of 20.1 per cent of the total issued ordinary share capital of IDG. Fyffes had held this investment stake for some five months but was not represented on the IDG Board.

IDG produced and marketed in Ireland, the UK and other member states of the EC a number of leading brands of whiskey; additionally it sold vodka and gin in Ireland only. Of particular importance were its whiskey brands, Powers Gold Label, Jameson, Paddy, Bushmills and Tullamore. These brands amounted to approximately 74 per cent of the Irish whiskey market. Guinness, at the time, was the second largest EC producer of spirits, and Allied Lyons PLC the third largest producer of spirits within the EC. Grand Metropolitan was the largest manufacturer and seller of drinks generally within the EC. On 28 June

* S J Berwin & Co acted in the UK for the Irish Distillers Group.

1988, IDG made an application pursuant to Article 3 of EC Regulation 17/62 complaining that the formation of the joint venture company G C & C Brands and the subsequent bid for IDG by that joint venture company constituted an infringement of Article 85(1) and Article 86 of the Treaty of Rome.

On 28 August 1988, the Commission initiated proceedings against Gilbeys and Cantrell & Cochrane, together with their respective parent companies, under Regulation 17 and informed the parties that it considered it appropriate in this case to take interim measures in the terms set out in a draft decision sent to the parties on 29 July 1988. In this draft decision the Commission found:

- There was a decision within Article 85(1) between G C & C Brands, Cantrell & Cochrane, Gilbeys, Grand Metropolitan, Allied Lyons and Guinness to make a bid for IDG and, if the bid were successful, jointly to distil IDG's brands of spirits and divide amongst themselves the distribution rights of those drinks.

- The relevant market was the whiskey market and not, as had been argued by the consortium members, the spirits market in general. In reaching this conclusion the Commission confirmed an earlier decision of 13 December 1985 that whiskey, gin and vodka are not considered by users as 'equivalent in view of their characteristics, price and intended use' and that 'a consumer looking for whiskey or gin will not readily buy a spirit from another category if no product belonging to the desired category is available'.

- The Commission considered that the relevant geographical market for whiskey was the whole of the EC.

- The Commission found the following restrictions of competition: it found that the agreement between Cantrell & Cochrane and Gilbeys and their parent companies to create the joint venture comany G C & C, the object of which was to acquire IDG and to divide up IDG brands between them, was a market-sharing agreement which distorted the competition that would normally exist between independent companies in the absence of the agreement.

  Furthermore, the Commission concluded that the effect of the agreement was to avoid bidding up the IDG share price so that the consortium members avoided paying a price that they would otherwise have to pay to acquire IDG. In this respect the arrangement constituted a bidding agreement which restricted competition within the meaning of Article 85(1). The

Commission looked by analogy at upward movements in the price of target companies in other large takeover battles, such as Rowntree/Suchard/Nestlé, British Sugar/Ferruzzi/Tate & Lyle, Distillers/Argyll/Guinness.

It also found the agreement between the parties jointly to operate IDG as a joint production company while dividing up the worldwide distribution rights of the brands to be a restriction of competition. Within this context the Commission referred to both the *Philip Morris* case and the *Carnaud/Sofreb* decision. The Commission emphasised that the creation of joint ventures immediately has a notable effect on the conduct of parent companies who have a significant holding in the joint venture and that where, as in this case, all the participating undertakings are actual competitors the agreement will restrict competition in the relevant market. The Commission looked at the facts of this case and emphasised that the restrictions on competition were unavoidable as the products in question, which were being divided between the joint venture, were jointly distilled and therefore each party was aware of the others' long-term marketing plans and production forecasts. The Commission also emphasised that there were possible 'spill-over effects' resulting from the operation of the joint venture in other areas of the bidders' activities.

The Commission saw the restrictions on competition as appreciable, taking into account the turnover of the groups of companies involved, the number of whiskey brands involved and IDG's particularly significant share of the Irish whiskey market (67.5 per cent).

- The Commission found no benefits of the proposed takeover which were indispensable to the transaction within the meaning of Article 85(3) of the Treaty of Rome. It emphasised the co-operative nature of the proposed running of the joint venture company and the fact that the Irish whiskey market had been growing in recent years but that because its principal competitors were the bidders, it was possible that in future bidders would have less interest in actively promoting their own Irish whiskey brands, which a completely independent company would not have.

Interim measures

The Commission thought that this was an appropriate case for interim measures to be taken because the only effective remedy in the event of an eventual final decision by the Commission prohibiting the takeover would be by divestiture of shares acquired by the offerors. During the interim period prior to the adoption of a final decision, if the offer were successful, IDG would be run by the offerors and there would be changes in the organisational personnel and the company which might seriously prejudice the ability of IDG to revert to running the company independently at a later date. The offerors would also have access to secret know-how of IDG.

The Commission therefore concluded that this was a case where the public interest required interim measures in order to prevent transfer of control of IDG to the bidders until such time as the Commission adopted a final decision.

Outcome of the Commission's decision

The consortium members were given two weeks from receipt of the Statement of Objections to make any written comments to the Commission. The Commission noted in its statement of objections that this time limit took account of the fact that the parties had already received and had been given an opportunity to comment on the complaint which led to the issue of the statement of objections. The parties were also given an opportunity to present their case orally and a date of 8 August was fixed for an oral hearing if the parties so wished. However, on 17 August 1988 it was announced that the parties to the joint ventures had decided to abandon not only their joint bid but also any other restrictive agreements between themselves. Undertakings were given by Grand Metropolitan, Allied Lyons and Guinness to the Commission, the effect of which was that although each party was free to bid independently for IDG (although Guinness announced that it did not intend to acquire IDG or any IDG assets), all collusive aspects of arrangements between parties which the Commission had formally objected to had been removed. Among the undertakings required from the parties in respect of any joint bidding the following were of particular significance:

- The parties agreed not to have joint negotiations or joint representations in dealing with the Public or Stock Exchange Authority.

- G C & C undertook to release Fyffes from its irrevocable undertakings to sell its shares to G C & C. Detailed rules and proceedings were established as to the manner in which the offeror could in future offer to acquire Fyffes shares in IDG which included a requirement that any offer by G C & C or its agents for the Fyffes shares had to be open for a minimum period of fourteen days and such offers had to be accepted by Fyffes after ten days had elapsed. Undertakings were also obtained that any party which successfully made a bid, which was subsequently declared unconditional, for IDG had to ensure that any disposal of IDG assets had to be by competitive tender on terms to be approved by the Commission for the purpose of ensuring that the competition rules of the Treaty of Rome were reserved. This was to ensure that the parties did not carry out *de facto* a joint sharing of brands in the future to which the Commission had objected in its statement of objections. The Commission also laid down stringent conditions to monitor the disposal of any IDG brands for a period of five years from the date of the undertakings.

Effects on UK mergers policy and takeover rules

The Commission's decision fully exposes the interaction between domestic competition, takeover rules and Articles 85 and 86.

The G C & C offer was at the relevant time under consideration by both the Office of Fair Trading in the UK under the provisions of the Fair Trading Act (since the relevant markets in Northern Ireland and the UK were affected by the bid) and in the Republic of Ireland under the provisions of the Irish Fair Trading Act. Both the Office of Fair Trading in London and the Fair Trading Commission in the Republic of Ireland were in the process of considering the bid.

At the time of the G C & C offer, no particular requirement had been imposed by the Takeover Panel in relation to a possible intervention by the Commission. The Takeover Panel rules provide for a bid to lapse in the event of a reference to the Monopolies and Mergers Commission under the Fair Trading Act but contain no similar provision for a bid to lapse in the event of the Commission's intervention, notwithstanding that at an early stage of the bid IDG had requested the Panel to make such a direction. Moreover, the English Takeover rules allow a bid to be revived after a reference to the Monopolies and Mergers Commission if and when the bid is cleared by the Monopolies and Mergers Commission, whereas there was no precedent as to whether, in the event of G C & C satisfying any objections raised by the Commission, it would be allowed to proceed with its bid, and if so on what terms.

If the Commission did allow a revised G C & C bid to proceed, did this prevent the Irish Trade Commission or the Office of Fair Trading from subsequently prohibiting the transaction on purely domestic grounds? This dilemma is, of course, at the very heart of the creation of a one-stop merger policy at an EC level.

The aftermath

The total share capital of G C & C was acquired by Gilbeys, which requested consent from the Takeover Panel to launch a fresh bid for IDG at a price of 400 pence per share. Immediately, therefore, the Commission's primary objection to the consortium bid, notably that it prevented the bidding up of the IDG share price, had proved correct. The question was, however, whether the UK Takeover Panel would permit the transaction to proceed since there was no precedent in the Takeover rules to cover such a situation following intervention by the Commission. On 19 August the Panel ruled that G C & C (now under its new ownership) could immediately make a fresh bid for Irish Distillers. It took the view that, in the light of the intervention of the Commission, shareholders in IDG had not been given a proper opportunity to consider the initial bid by G C & C. It therefore exercised its discretion to permit the new bid to be made by G C & C without waiting for the normal twelve-month period to launch a new bid under the Takeover rules.

On 2 September, Pernod-Ricard and IDG issued a joint statement in which they said that talks were proceeding for an agreed bid by Pernod-Ricard for IDG. Over the weekend of 3 and 4 September Pernod-Ricard indicated to a number of shareholders that it would make an offer for IDG at 450 (Irish) pence per share, if it could obtain in advance irrevocable commitments to accept the proposed offer from the holders of shares which, together with those shares already held by Pernod-Ricard, would represent over 50 per cent of the shares in IDG.

In their decision of 19 August, the Panel had ruled that the new G C & C bid could not be increased unless a competing bid was made. On 2 September, at the time of the Pernod-Ricard IDG initiative, G C & C indicated that it would increase its bids for IDG if permitted to do so by the Takeover Panel and contended that the Pernod-Ricard initiative constituted a competing 'offer' which should allow it to increase its own offer.

On 5 September Pernod-Ricard announced a bid for Irish Distillers and contended that it had received irrevocable undertakings which, together with shares already held by it, represented over 50 per cent of the share capital. Immediately afterwards the Panel Executive allowed

G C & C to increase its bid to 525 pence per share. At approximately the same time a dispute became apparent between Pernod-Ricard and Fyffes as to whether Fyffes had irrevocably committed its 20 per cent stake in IDG to Pernod. There followed litigation in the Irish Court as to whether there had been a binding irrevocable oral commitment.

Meanwhile G C & C also complained to the Commission, claiming the arrangements between IDG and Pernod-Ricard had the object and effect of eliminating competition in the bidding process from G C & C and any other bidder for IDG, the object and effect of which was to prevent all IDG shareholders from having the opportunity of considering whether to accept G C & C's higher offer of 525 pence per share. Interim measures were requested from the Commission. IDG submitted that there was no infringement of Article 85(1) of the Treaty of Rome by the IDG/Pernod arrangement. The Takeover Panel's original decision on 17 August restricted G C & C's right to increase their bid (which had been stated to be 'final') to circumstances where there was a competing offer. No such offer had been made. Therefore, G C & C was not in a position to increase its offer.

Finally, G C & C brands complained to the Takeover Panel that the manner in which IDG/Pernod had obtained its irrevocable acceptances was contrary to the Takeover Panel rules, and therefore those who had given the irrevocable acceptances should be freed from their ties.

The outcome

The Commission ruled that the 'shut-out' by Pernod and IDG did not infringe Article 85 of the Treaty of Rome. It provided G C & C an opportunity to make further observations on their complaint before taking a final decision but as a result of other developments this was not pursued by G C & C.

The Takeover Panel ruled that, although a limited number of Pernod-Ricard's irrevocable acceptances may have been obtained on a basis which questionably was open to criticism, the procedural irregularities were not such as to warrant setting the acceptances aside.

The Irish Court held that Fyffes had irrevocably accepted by means of an oral contract the Pernod-Ricard bid of 450 pence during the week of 3–4 September.

On 16 November 1988, the Irish Trade Minister prohibited the G C & C bid proceeding on the basis that it operated against the general good in the Republic of Ireland. The Pernod-Ricard bid was also prohibited, but the Minister's order laid down a number of conditions as to the future conduct of the IDG business, which, if Pernod-Ricard was prepared to comply with them, would entitle Pernod-Ricard to acquire IDG. Pernod-Ricard agreed to the conditions.

Conclusion

The IDG affair illustrates a unique interplay between Community and domestic competition and takeover rules. It illustrates the importance of recognising how Community competition rules can be used both as a shield and as a sword both by the poachers and by the gamekeepers in the takeover scenario. It also serves to illustrate how in the lead up to 1992 numerous adjustments will have to take place in domestic legislation both in the UK and in other member states to regulate the interplay of domestic laws and rules to the application of Community rules, whether in the form of Articles 85 and 86 of the Treaty of Rome or a one-stop merger regulation.

Domestic competition laws and EC merger control in France, West Germany, Spain and Italy

An English company acquiring an interest in a company established in another member state will always have to consider the possible application and interaction of EC and domestic competition laws. At present, Articles 85 and 86 of the Treaty of Rome represent the only legal basis for the Commission to intervene on competition grounds, and competition authorities in member states where the proposed transaction may have a potential effect on competition remain competent to investigate the transaction in accordance with their own domestic competition laws.

If and when a merger regulation is adopted by the Council of Ministers there will remain circumstances in which concurrent jurisdiction of domestic and EC competition laws will continue to apply. Working on the basis that the matters of principle on this question remain as currently drafted in the Draft Merger Regulation, member states will remain competent to apply their own domestic competition laws where the transaction does not come within the scope of the Draft Merger Regulation and the Commission has recently indicated that it may make provision in the Regulation for this competence of member states to be declared exclusive following clearance by the Commission.

A merger (all forms of merger, acquisition and takeover, whether they involve the acquisition of controlling or minority interests in shares or assets) will not come within the scope of the Draft Merger Regulation in any of the following circumstances:

- If the aggregate turnover of all the undertakings concerned in the merger is less than 1,000 million ecu (approximately £650 million). The Commission has proposed that this figure is doubled to 2,000 million ecu.

- If there are not at least two undertakings involved in the merger whose community-wide turnover is more than 100 million ecu (approximately £66 million) each. The Commission has proposed that this figure also be doubled.

- If all the undertakings involved achieve more than three-quarters of their aggregate Community-wide turnover in any one individual member state. The Commission has proposed that this be decreased to two-thirds of aggregate turnover.

- If control of the target company does not pass as a result of the merger.

- If the object or effect of the merger is to co-ordinate the competitive behaviour of independent undertakings.

In all the above circumstances, although the Draft Merger Regulation will not apply, Articles 85 and 86 may be applicable, as will the domestic competition laws of individual member states.

Where a merger falls within the scope of the Draft Merger Regulation and is duly notified to the Commission, the Commission may, when authorising it as 'compatible with the Common Market', attach conditions and may also empower those member states directly concerned to apply their own national competition legislation 'to ensure effective competition in local markets within their respective territories' (Article 8(2) of the present draft). Such a decision must be taken by the Commission within one month of the initiation of proceedings under the Draft Regulation.

Subject to the above, the Commission will have sole competence to take the decisions provided for in the Draft Merger Regulation, to the exclusion of national competition authorities. However, as there are so many exceptions, even in the case of very large companies, it remains of crucial importance for UK businesses to recognise their potential double exposure under EC and domestic competition laws and to familiarise themselves fully with the requirements of the target company's home member state as they will apply to the circumstances of the merger in the context of the commercial and market background.

We asked four leading firms of lawyers, Gide Loyrette Nouel in France, Modest Gundisch Landry in West Germany, Gomez-Acebo & Pombo in Spain and Studio Legale Bisconti in Italy, to advise on a number of specific questions in relation to the competition considerations that arise under their domestic competition laws for a UK corporation wishing to acquire either a minority interest or a majority stake in a company within their respective local jurisdictions, where the proposed acquisition is likely to result in an increase in concentration in the relevant product market.

The questions were as follows:

1. Is there a system of local merger control and, if so, what is its legal basis?

2. To what type of transactions do your merger control rules apply?

3. Does the structure of the transaction affect the application of the domestic competition rules? Does it matter whether a minority or majority stake is being acquired?

4. How are the competition rules enforced?

5. How will the UK company be able to assess the likelihood of its proposed transaction being prohibited on competition grounds? What criteria are applied?

6. What is the timing for intervention by domestic competition authorities?

7. What is the relationship with EC merger control provisions?

These are the answers we received.

1. Is there a system of local merger control and, if so, what is its legal basis?

France

Yes. French merger control is governed by a French Ordinance dated 1 December 1986, Title V, articles 38–44 (the Ordinance). This replaced earlier merger control legislation dating back to 1977. The law subjects to control those mergers which may hinder competition in the relevant market in France.

West Germany

Yes. Merger control has existed in West Germany since 1973; it was originally introduced by the second amendment to the Law against Restraints of Competition. The relevant law is the law against restrictions on competition (the competition law). This law prohibits mergers which create or reinforce a dominant market position unless the undertakings concerned can demonstrate that the merger results in improvements in competitive conditions which outweigh the disadvantages of market dominance.

Spain

The only competition law currently in force in Spain is Law 110/1963 of 20 July 1983 which does *not* deal with merger control, other than for a formal registration requirement. This law is, however, to be substituted by a new competition law which contains specific provisions for the control of mergers, the terms of which are set out in a draft bill pending before the Spanish Parliament. This draft bill, which provides the basis of the present analysis, provides a procedure for investigation and prohibition of mergers which imperil effective competition in the relevant market in which the merger is to operate.

Italy

At present Italy does not have any domestic anti-trust or merger control legislation of general application, although there are laws regulating unfair competition and covenants not to compete in the general provisions of the Civil Code (Article 2595 and following). There are also special rules in force regulating the establishment of dominant positions in the field of newspapers and other periodical publications (Law No. 416 of 5 August 1981 as subsequently implemented and/or amended). The Italian Council of Ministers has recently approved and submitted to Parliament a bill containing rules for the protection of competition and of the market ('the Bill'). There are in addition other bills pending before the Italian Parliament for regulation of groups of companies, takeover bids and ownership by industrial companies of banks which are likely to have some impact on concentration control. The present analysis is based on the present draft of the Bill, which, if enacted, will establish the basic competition rules for the control of mergers in Italy.

General Advice

At present the UK company will not encounter significant merger control restrictions in Spain or Italy although this position is likely to change between now and 1992. In West Germany and France, the UK company will encounter well established systems of merger control regulation.

2. To what type of transactions do your merger control rules apply?

France

According to Article 40 of the Ordinance, 'All merger proposals and all mergers completed within the previous three months *may* be submitted to the Minister of Economy by the firms concerned . . .'. Merger control provisions apply only when the parties to or subject to the agreement, or firms which are economically connected with them, together account for over 25 per cent of purchases, sales or other transactions in the domestic goods, products or services markets or in a substantial part of such markets, or have a turnover (excluding taxes) of over 7 billion francs (approximately £648 million), provided that at least two of the companies which are parties to the merger have a turnover of at least 2 billion francs each (approximately £185 million) during the same period. As far as the market thresholds are concerned, the relevant market territory is to be considered to be either the national market or a substantial part thereof.

West Germany   In West Germany certain mergers have to be pre-notified to the Federal Cartel Authority whereas other categories of transaction are not required to be notified until post-merger completion.

The Federal Cartel Office is required to be notified of a merger 'without undue delay' if any of the following apply:

- The merger results in, or increases a previously existing market share of at least 20 per cent in any market within West Germany

- An undertaking participating in the merger has a market share of at least 20 per cent in any other market within West Germany

- The participating enterprises collectively have at any time during the fiscal year immediately preceding the merger at least 10,000 employees or sales of at least DM 500 million (approximately £155 million)

Market shares in markets outside West Germany are disregarded. The number of employees and sales are computed on a worldwide basis.

Notice of a merger plan must be given to the Federal Cartel Office before its completion where:

- The consolidated sales of one or more of the participating undertakings during the last preceding fiscal year amounted to DM 2,000 million (approximately £620 million)

- The consolidated sales of two or more of the participating enterprises during such period amounted to DM 1,000 million (approximately £310 million)

In other cases, although notice of a merger plan may be given before completion if the participating enterprises so decide (voluntary pre-merger notification), control is exercised *ex post facto* although it is open to the Federal Cartel Office to intervene of its own initiative at any time prior to completion of the merger.

A merger is not subject to the West German competition rules (although it is still subject to notification) if the participating undertakings and their affiliates during the last fiscal year preceding the merger collectively had worldwide sales of less than DM 500 million (approximately £155 million). The effect on competition of such mergers is treated as insignificant. A merger is also not subject to prohibition if, during the fiscal year immediately preceding the merger, the acquired undertakings did not have a turnover exceeding DM 50 million (approximately £15,500,000). Small and medium-sized enterprises may therefore avoid the application of the West German merger control rules as long as they fall within these exemptions.

Spain   The new draft Spanish competition bill will apply to any company merger or takeover of one or several companies by another person, company or group of companies, where any of them is established in Spain if one of the following applies:

- The participating companies control one quarter or more of the domestic market for a certain product or service, or one of the companies previously controls that percentage

- The joint global turnover of the companies exceeds, in the accounting year preceding the merger, the sum of Pta 20,000 million (approximately £100 million)

Italy   The Bill provides for control of mergers other than in cases where the aggregate *Italian* turnover of the participating undertakings is less than 500 billion lire (approximately £220 million) or unless the Italian turnover of the enterprise to be acquired is less than 50 billion lire (approximately £22 million). The concentration control provisions will apply, in any event, if the share of the participating undertakings in the relevant Italian market is 40 per cent or more.

General Advice   *The UK company will encounter a considerable variety of qualifying financial limits applied in the different member states and the manner in which those financial limits are calculated, in particular in relation to whether the financial limits are calculated by reference to domestic turnover or international turnover. There are also significant differences in the levels of concentration at which the domestic competition rules will apply.*

3.   Does the structure of the transaction affect the application of the domestic competition rules? Does it matter whether a minority or majority stake is being acquired?

France   The definition of a merger in the Ordinance is wider than that of a 'concentration' contained in the Draft Regulation. The Ordinance provides that 'A merger is the result of any type of act, which has the effect of transferring legal or beneficial ownership of all or part of the assets, rights and obligations of a firm or which has the object or effect of enabling a firm or a combination of firms to directly or indirectly exercise a decisive influence over one or several other firms'. This definition in the Ordinance applies merger control to a wide variety of transactions including financial commitments between undertakings, interlocking directorates, groupings of firms and the acquisition both of majority and minority shareholdings. Therefore, even a 30 per cent acquisition of shares in a French company is likely to be deemed a merger within the meaning of this definition, and the acquisition of 51 per cent or 100 per cent of shares will almost certainly fall within its scope of application.

West Germany

The West German merger rules are expressed to apply to mergers between enterprises, including acquisitions of assets or shares, the formation of joint ventures and other transactions as defined in the legal provisions. Acquisitions of shares in another enterprise constitute a merger if such shares alone or taken together with other shares already held equal 25 per cent or 50 per cent of the voting capital of the other enterprise or result in a majority interest. The acquisition of less than 25 per cent of shares can be deemed to be a merger in certain limited circumstances. As a general rule, the merger control provisions will apply to the successive acquisition of shares each time a threshold of 25 per cent, 50 per cent and above 50 per cent of the share capital is reached.

The acquisition of shares by one undertaking in another also constitutes a merger if such shares alone, or together with other shares already held, do not equal 25 per cent of the voting capital of the other enterprise but the acquiring undertaking is afforded by agreement, articles of association, or resolution, a legal position equivalent to that of a shareholder in a stock corporation holding more than 25 per cent of the voting capital. It is possible that in future legislation the 25 per cent threshold will be reduced to 10 per cent.

The definition of merger also extends to a variety of other legal relationships including the creation of a new joint venture company, interlocking directorates, and the creation by contract of any other relationship by virtue of which one enterprise exercises directly or indirectly a 'dominating' influence over another enterprise.

Spain

The present Spanish draft competition law does not define a merger of companies or a takeover. It provides in general terms that 'any merger or takeover of one or several enterprises which can or might affect the Spanish market has to be notified to the Competition Service at least one month before its coming into effect'. The relevant Spanish legislation relating to mergers (such as the Spanish Companies Law, Code of Commerce, Law of Co-operatives, Civil Code, Law of Associations and Co-operation between Companies, Law of Temporary Associations of Companies) provides that a merger can take place by absorption, by incorporation, by liquidation of a company, sale and purchase of shares, sale and purchase of assets, sale and purchase of a company or through joint ventures.

A merger of companies or a takeover is therefore defined in very general terms and extends to any assumption of *de facto* control by one company or undertaking over another. It includes the acquisition of a minority as well as a majority stake.

Italy

The definition of 'concentration' in Article 5 of the draft bill is substantially the same as that contained in the Draft Regulation. Therefore, the acquisition of a controlling interest, or direct or indirect control of the whole or parts of an undertaking, or the formation by two or more undertakings of a joint undertaking constitute a merger under the draft Italian legislation.

General Advice

The UK company will find that there is no uniform definition of what constitutes a merger under the domestic competition laws. Generally, however, the acquisition of a minority interest which provides de facto *influence or control is likely to fall within the scope of application of domestic merger control.*

4. How are the competition rules enforced?

France

Notification to the relevant French authorities is not mandatory. The French Minister of the Economy and the Minister in charge of the specific economic field related to the proposed merger have primary responsibility for the enforcement of the merger provisions in the Ordinance. If a notification is made to the French Minister of the Economy and he does not respond within two months of receipt of the notification, the proposed notification is deemed to have been approved. If, however, the Minister is minded to take an adverse view of the merger he must first refer the case to the French Competition Council. He is required to inform the parties of the decision to refer the case to the French Competition Council, at which point the deadline for a final decision is extended to six months from the date of notification. If the Competition Council considers that the merger falls within the terms of the Ordinance, it is required to make an assessment on the basis of legal documents and details of the transaction submitted to it as to whether the transaction is likely to have an anti-competitive effect in the relevant market and, if so, whether the benefits to the economy resulting from the transaction outweigh any such anti-competitive consequences. The merger can be prohibited by the Minister or allowed, subject to conditions. A decision of the Minister of the Economy is subject to appeal by way of judicial review to the French Courts.

It is only if the parties refuse to obey the Minister of the Economy's decision that penalties can be imposed. Before imposing a fine in such circumstances, the Minister of the Economy is required to consult the

French Competition Council and is only permitted to impose a penalty within the limits of the advice issued by the Council. The maximum fine is set at 5 per cent of the relevant undertaking's turnover in France during the last complete financial year.

West Germany

Mergers policy is administered in West Germany by the Federal Cartel Office. The Federal Cartel Office cannot exercise discretionary powers in its examination of the competition considerations. Its decisions are open to judicial review by the Courts on application by the undertakings concerned. The Federal Cartel Office has far-reaching powers to investigate whether a transaction constitutes a merger and, if so, whether a merger creates or strengthens a market-dominating position. Its powers include the power of entry, search and seizure. It may request the participating enterprises to disclose certain information in addition to that contained in the notification, and it may also ask third parties to provide information on the economic situation.

It is open to the Federal Minister of the Economy, after obtaining the expert opinion of the Federal Monopoly Commission, to allow a merger prohibited by the Federal Cartel Office if the Minister considers that the adverse effects of a merger are compensated by overall economic avantages; or an overriding public interest justifies the merger. It is exceptional in West Germany for the Minister to invoke these powers.

Spain

The new draft Spanish competition law has maintained the same institutions created by the Competition Law of 1963, for the enforcement of the competition rules. These institutions are the Competition Tribunal and the Competition Service, which are responsible respectively for carrying out the first and second stages of the proceedings, the Competition Tribunal being the superior body to the Competition Service.

The Competition Service forms part of the Ministry of Economy and Finance. It is the principal administrative authority in competition matters and is the body responsible for co-ordinating with the Commission the application of the Spanish competition rules and EC competition rules. The Competition Service must be notified at least three months prior to a qualifying merger coming into effect. Once a merger has been notified, the Competition Service appoints an Examiner and a Secretary and it is required to investigate the merger in accordance with its own procedures.

The Competition Tribunal, which *enforces* the Spanish co-operation rules, forms part of the Ministry of Economy and Finance and consists of a chairman and eight members. It is competent to hear all matters entrusted to it by law, which includes consideration of whether a merger is anti-competitive. It is also charged with applying Articles 85 and 86 of the EC Treaty in Spain. The Competition Tribunal has decision-making power including the taking of any permissive, prohibitive or conditional decisions. A decision of the Competition Tribunal normally exhausts all administrative procedures in application of the competition rules.

If the Competition Service considers that competition is affected by a qualifying merger, it must within one month submit a report to the Spanish Competition Tribunal which is required within three months to submit a report to the Minister of the Economy who in turn submits the report to the Spanish Council of Ministers. The latter must then within three months decide whether to oppose the merger, prohibit it, or order that appropriate measures be taken for the maintenance or re-establishment of conditions of effective competition in the relevant Spanish market.

Italy

Under the Bill before the Italian Parliament, the new competition laws will be administered by a Competition Authority. If the Authority finds that the proposed concentration is likely to prejudice competition, it will prohibit the concentration, unless the increased concentration can be justified by reference to the maintenance of international competitiveness of the enterprises or in order to increase or improve qualitatively production or distribution, or to promote technological research and progress, in the interest of the national economy.

General Advice

Although the laws are primarily administered and enforced by competition authorities there is, at a final stage, intervention at a political level, although the likelihood of such intervention will vary from member state to member state. Therefore it may be necessary for the UK company to lobby at a political level in these jurisdictions as well as to take local advice on relevant competition law considerations.

5.   How will the UK company be able to assess the likelihood of its proposed transaction being prohibited on competition grounds? What criteria are applied?

France

As noted above, in determining whether to permit a qualifying merger to proceed, the French Competition Council has to ascertain whether the proposed merger hinders competition or, if applicable, determine whether the benefits to the economy sufficiently outweigh any anticompetitive effects. The Ordinance refers specifically to 'the creation or strengthening of a dominant position' as an instance of the most dangerous case of abusive concentration, but otherwise it is for the

Commission to work out in individual decisions when, in a specific case, there is a hindrance to competition. In determining whether there is any countervailing benefit to the economy from the merger, the Commission takes into account increased international competition resulting from the merger and also factors such as the merger bringing about the recovery of undertakings encountering financial difficulties, the rationalisation of manufacturing capacity or a decrease in costs.

West Germany

In West Germany complex rules are administered by the Federal Cartel Office to determine the likely effects on competition of the merger. Of pivotal importance in these rules are the definition of the relevant market and certain statutory presumptions as to the existence of a monopoly or oligopoly situation.

- Monopoly: The legislation deems an enterprise to hold a market-dominating position if it is without competitors or not subject to substantial competition, or if it has a 'superior market position' in relation to its competitors.

- Oligopoly: Each of two or more undertakings is deemed to possess a market-dominating position if there is no substantial competition between such undertakings and if such undertakings jointly hold a market-dominating position.

- General statutory presumptions of market dominance: These presumptions are based on the market shares of the participating enterprises active in the relevant market.
  An undertaking is presumed to be market-dominating and there is a presumption of monopoly if it has a market share of one-third or more.
  Three or fewer undertakings having the highest market shares are presumed to be market-dominating if together they have a market share of one half or more.
  Five or fewer undertakings having the highest market shares are presumed to be market-dominating if together they have a market share of two-thirds or more, unless these participating undertakings demonstrate that the competitive situation is such that substantial competition between the oligopolists can be expected to prevail in the future or that the oligopolists together will not hold an improved market position in relation to their competitors.

- The law also defines certain other statutory presumptions in relation to vertical and conglomerate mergers where undertakings enter markets dominated by small or medium-sized enterprises, acquire market-dominating enterprises, or merge with other large enterprises.

Spain

The general test applied in Spain by the Spanish Competition Service is whether in the future (even if not immediately) the proposed merger is likely to imperil the maintenance of effective competition in the relevant product market. The new draft law defines five relevant circumstances to determine whether a particular situation may result in a merger having an adverse effect on the maintenance of effective competition. The relevant criteria are the effects of the merger on market structure, the possibilities of choice for suppliers, distributors and consumers, the economic and financial powers of the participating undertakings as a result of the merger, the structure of the offer on supply and demand, and the merger's effects on external competition.

Italy

Under the Italian Bill the only test proposed is whether the concentration constitutes an abuse of a dominant position which may have a prejudicial effect on competition within the Italian market. If there is such a prejudicial effect the merger is subject to prohibition and the other measures provided for in the Bill. The Italian legislation does not define in more detail what constitutes an abuse of a dominant position or a prejudicial effect on competition. The Bill specifically provides that its provisions are to be interpreted in accordance with principles of EC competition law.

The Bill provides that, in the event of a participating undertaking being an EC undertaking, where its member state of incorporation discriminates in its own domestic legislation against acquisitions by Italian enterprises in that country, the concentration can be prohibited by the Council of Ministers on these grounds alone. Acquisitions and concentrations by undertakings from non-EC countries may also be prohibited in the essential interest of the national economy (Article 26).

General Advice

It is clear that West Germany stands alone in defining statutory presumptions as to when a merger may have an anti-competitive effect. The competition-based criteria in all four countries can be compared with a far wider criteria applied by the Office of Fair Trading under Section 84 of the 1973 Fair Trading Act in English merger control legislation. It is clear from the advice received from the local lawyers that the UK company must have a clear grasp of the nature of the relevant market in the country in which it wishes to make the acquisition, and of the effects the transaction is likely to have on the maintenance of effective competition in that market.

6. What is the timing for intervention by domestic competition authorities?

France

As explained above, if the Minister of the Economy does not respond to a notification of a merger within two months of the receipt of the notification, the proposed merger will be deemed to have been approved. Otherwise the deadline for the Minister's reply is extended to six months from the date of notification. In the event of the Minister not replying within six months, the merger is deemed to be approved.

West Germany

In the case of a mandatory or voluntary pre-merger notification, the Federal Cartel Office has a period of four months from the date of receipt of the complete notification to investigate and to prohibit the merger, provided it has informed the notifying parties in writing within one month after receipt of the notification that the merger is to be investigated. If the Federal Cartel Office does not give such notice within one month after receipt of the notification, it forfeits the right to investigate and prohibit the merger. In the case of a post-merger notification, the Federal Cartel Office may investigate and prohibit the merger within one year after receipt of a completed notification. There may therefore be considerable advantage in notification to avoid continuing uncertainty. These time limits may be extended by mutual agreement between the Federal Cartel Office and the participating undertakings.

Spain

As we note above, under the draft Spanish legislation, the proposed merger has to be notified to the Spanish Competition Service three months before it is to be effected if, as a consequence of the proposed merger, the market share or turnover limits are likely to be reached. In the event of failure to notify, the Minister of the Economy may impose fines of up to 5 per cent of the undertaking's turnover. If the Spanish Competition Service concludes within a period of one month that the merger may hinder the maintenance of effective competition in the relevant market, it submits a report to the Spanish Competition Tribunal which then has one month to review the merger. The report of the Spanish Competition Tribunal is transmitted to the Spanish government. The Spanish Council of Ministers then has a period of three months to decide what action, if any, to take.

Italy

Concentrations falling within the scope of the Italian merger control must be notified in advance. Failure to notify qualifying concentrations renders the enterprise in breach of the competition rules and liable to fines. The Competition Authority is required, within thirty days of receipt of such a notification, to initiate a formal investigation. Public takeover bids which may result in a concentration are required to be notified to the Competition Authority at the same time as the bid is notified to the National Commission on Companies and the Stock Exchange (CONSOB). The Authority is then required to inform the purchaser that it has commenced a formal investigation within fifteen days from receipt of the notification. If these periods have expired without a formal investigation having been announced, the concentration is deemed to be cleared unless the information supplied by the notifying enterprises is subsequently found to be 'grossly inexact', incomplete or false.

If the Authority does not issue any prohibition within forty-five days from the start of the formal investigation, the concentration is deemed to be cleared. The forty-five day period may, however, be extended if, in the course of the investigation, the enterprises do not supply information requested by the Authority, which is within their control.

General Advice

In the event that the acquisition may create a potential competition problem in the member states concerned, the UK company may have to wait up to six months for clearance of the transaction. While there is considerable diversity in the time-limits between the different member states, in general (other than in the case of post-notification mergers in West Germany) six months is the maximum time required for clearance, although it should be noted that in all countries notification is required before completion of the transaction in certain circumstances.

7. What is the relationship with EC merger control provisions?

We asked each one of the local lawyers for their opinion as to how their own competition legislation or proposed legislation would treat the double jeopardy scenario described on pp. 125–7 where the UK company's proposed acquisition has to be cleared both by the Commission and the relevant domestic competition authorities.

France

Gide Loyrette Nouel advise that if the French authorities were empowered by the Commission to apply French merger control legislation, under Article 8(2) of the Draft Regulation the French legislation would be applied in the usual way. However, if in application of the Draft Regulation, the Commission were to declare a concentration falling within the scope of application of the Draft Regulation compatible with the Common Market, or grant an exemption on the basis that the proposed merger improves production and distribution, promotes technical or economic progress, or improves the competitive structure within the Common Market in a manner outweighing the damage to competition, such a decision by the Commission would bar the French competition authorities from applying their own competition rules. There is no other French legislation which deals with the possibility of conflicts of jurisdiction between the French and the EC competition rules.

West Germany   Modest Gundisch and Landry advise that once a merger falling within the scope of application of the Draft Regulation is cleared by the Commission the Federal Cartel Office has no further power to intervene. If the Commission has commenced proceedings but approval has not yet been given, a decision by the Federal Cartel Office cannot be made. If the Commission has been notified of the merger, but the Commission has not at the time of notification to the Federal Cartel Office defined its position, the Federal Cartel Office must stay its proceedings. Changes to West German law are not necessary to take account of the Draft Regulation since the Regulation is supra-national-law that takes precedence over domestic legal provisions. On the other hand, the Draft Regulation is likely to require changes to the West German competition rules with regard to those mergers that do not fall within the scope of application of the Draft Regulation. Owing to the fact that the size criteria for the application of West German cartel law are considerably smaller than those under the Draft Regulation, there are likely to be numerous cases where West German merger control will continue to apply. However, the precise relationship between national and EC competition laws is a matter of considerable debate and, in the past, conflicts between the decisions of the Commission and the Federal Cartel Office have been resolved as follows:

- In cases where the Commission prohibits a merger because the agreements or concerted practices violate Article 85(1) or Article 86, such prohibition takes precedence over any decision of the Federal Cartel Office.

- In cases where the Commission grants an exemption for a merger pursuant to Article 85(3), it is a matter of some controversy as to whether the Federal Cartel Office may nevertheless prohibit the exempted merger as far as it affects the West German market. The Federal Cartel Office has claimed but never exercised such power although Modest Gundisch and Landry consider it doubtful whether the Cartel Office does have such power.

- In cases where the Commission has decided not to intervene, the Federal Cartel Office may prohibit the merger as far as it affects the West German market.

Spain   Gomez-Acebo & Pombo advise that the Spanish competition authorities will not apply the Spanish legislation to concentrations having a Community dimension unless expressly empowered to do so by the Commission in accordance with the provisions of the last sentence of

Article 8(2) – notably when a notified concentration is considered compatible with the Common Market, but conditions for effective competition in local markets in the territory of Spain demand the application of the Spanish rules.

In the Spanish Draft Competition Bill there is no provision regulating the simultaneous notification of a merger to the Spanish Competition Service and the Commission. However, according to Article 46 of the Draft Bill, the Spanish Competition Service can suspend its consideration of a merger when it is established that the same matter is being considered by the Competition Directorate of the Commission. This stay of the Spanish proceedings lasts until the Commission has concluded its consideration of the merger. Although there is no other Spanish legislation regulating conflicts of jurisdiction between the Spanish and EC competition rules, it is likely that any such conflict of jurisdiction would be solved in Spanish law according to the general principle of the priority of directly effective Community laws over any conflicting provisions of domestic law, including decisions in application of the Spanish competition rules.

Italy

Studio Legale Bisconti advise that if, prior to or in the course of the proceedings before the Italian competition authority, proceedings have been commenced under EC competition rules, the authority will not act unless and until the EC proceedings are concluded. The Bill provides for the priority of Community competition rules wherever a proposed concentration falls within the scope of application of both EC and domestic rules. In these circumstances the Bill excludes the possibility of a merger having to satisfy a double barrier test if the Community authorities have issued a favourable decision on the merger and, as a result, the merger is not subject to double jeopardy in the event of a favourable Commission decision. The position is, however, different if the proposed concentration falls outside the scope of application of both the Draft Regulation and Articles 85 and 86. In such circumstances, if the merger meets the Italian threshold requirements it would be subject to notification to the authority and therefore subject to the Italian rules on merger control.

Conclusion

In the development of a 1992 strategy for growth by acquisition, merger control provisions in EC member states must be fully considered along with their interaction with the Community merger control provisions. The UK company will find that, although in all the member states in which it may wish to proceed with the acquisition the principle of supremacy of Community law over domestic law is applied, there remains within Community law limits considerable scope for the practical application of domestic competition rules particularly to mergers between small and medium-sized enterprises or mergers which have a more significant impact on competition in the domestic market than in the EC market at large.

Pre-planning for 1992 must therefore take account of how to deal with domestic competition rules as well as the Community regime.

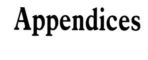

Appendices

Appendix I: Selected legislation and other material

Treaty of Rome clauses on freedom of establishment and provision of services

Article 52

Within the framework of the provisions set out below, restrictions on the freedom of establishment of nationals of a member state in the territory of another member state shall be abolished by progressive stages in the course of the transitional period. Such progressive abolition shall also apply to restrictions on the setting up of agencies, branches or subsidiaries by nationals of any member state established in the territory of any member state.

Freedom of establishment shall include the right to take up and pursue activities as self-employed persons and to set up and manage undertakings, in particular companies or firms within the meaning of the second paragraph of Article 58, under the conditions laid down for its own nationals by the law of the country where such establishment is effective, subject to the provisions of the Chapter relating to capital.

Article 53

Member states shall not introduce any new restrictions on the right of establishment in their territories of nationals of other member states, save as otherwise provided in this Treaty.

Article 54

1. Before the end of the first stage, the Council shall, acting unanimously on a proposal from the Commission and after consulting the Economic and Social Committee and the Assembly, draw up a general programme for the abolition of existing restric-

tions on freedom of establishment within the Community. The Commission shall submit its proposals to the Council during the first two years of the first stage.

The programme shall set out the general conditions under which freedom of establishment is to be attained in the case of each type of activity and in particular the stages by which it is to be attained.

2.   In order to implement this general programme or, in the absence of such programme, in order to achieve a stage in attaining freedom of establishment as regards a particular activity, the Council shall on a proposal from the Commission and after consulting the Economic and Social Committee and the Assembly, issue directives, acting unanimously until the end of the first stage and by a qualified majority thereafter.

3.   The Council and the Commission shall carry out the duties devolving upon them under the preceding provisions, in particular:

(a) by according, as a general rule, priority treatment to activities where freedom of establishment makes a particularly valuable contribution to the development of production and trade;

(b) by ensuring close cooperation between the competent authorities in the member states in order to ascertain the particular situation within the Community of the various activities concerned;

(c) by abolishing those administrative procedures and practices, whether resulting from national legislation or from agreements previously concluded between member states, the maintenance of which would form an obstacle to freedom of establishment;

(d) by ensuring that workers of one member state employed in the territory of another member state may remain in that territory for the purpose of taking up activities therein as self-employed persons, where they satisfy the conditions which they would be required to satisfy if they were entering that state at the time when they intended to take up such activities;

(e) by enabling a national of one member state to acquire and use land and buildings situated in the territory of another member state, in so far as this does not conflict with the principles laid down in Article 39(2);

(f) by effecting the progressive abolition of restrictions on freedom of establishment in every branch of activity under consideration, both as regards the conditions for setting up agencies, branches or subsidiaries in the territory of a member state and as regards the conditions governing the entry of personnel belonging to the main establishment into managerial or supervisory posts in such agencies, branches or subsidiaries;

(g) by co-ordinating to the necessary extent the safeguards which, for the protection of the interests of members and others, are required by member states of companies or firms within the meaning of the second paragraph of Article 58 with a view to making such safeguards equivalent throughout the Community;

(h) by satisfying themselves that the conditions of establishment are not distorted by aids granted by member states.

Article 55

The provisions of this Chapter shall not apply, so far as any given member state is concerned, to activities which in that state are connected, even occasionally, with the exercise of official authority.

The Council may, acting by a qualified majority on a proposal from the Commission, rule that the provisions of this Chapter shall not apply to certain activities.

Article 56

1. The provisions of this Chapter and measures taken in pursuance thereof shall not prejudice the applicability of provisions laid down by law, regulation or administrative action providing for special treatment for foreign nationals on grounds of public policy, public security or public health.

2. Before the end of the transitional period, the Council shall, acting unanimously on a proposal from the Commission and after consulting the Assembly, issue directives for the coordination of the aforementioned provisions laid down by law, regulation or administrative action. After the end of the second stage, however, the Council shall, acting by a qualified majority on a proposal

from the Commission, issue directives for the coordination of such provisions as, in each member state, are a matter for regulation or administrative action.

Article 57

1. In order to make it easier for persons to take up and pursue activities as self-employed persons, the Council shall, on a proposal from the Commission and after consulting the Assembly, acting unanimously during the first stage and by a qualified majority thereafter, issue directives for the mutual recognition of diplomas, certificates and other evidence of formal qualifications.

2. For the same purpose, the Council shall, before the end of the transitional period, acting on a proposal from the Commission and after consulting the Assembly, issue directives for the coordination of the provisions laid down by law, regulation or administrative action in member states concerning the taking up and pursuit of activities as self-employed persons. Unanimity shall be required on matters which are the subject of legislation in at least one member state and measures concerned with the protection of savings, in particular the granting of credit and the exercise of the banking profession, and with the conditions governing the exercise of the medical and allied and pharmaceutical professions in the various member states. In other cases, the Council shall act unanimously during the first stage and by a qualified majority thereafter.

3. In the case of the medical and allied and pharmaceutical professions, the progressive abolition of restrictions shall be dependent upon coordination of the conditions for their exercise in the various member states.

Article 58

Companies or firms formed in accordance with the law of a member state and having their registered office, central administration or principal place of business within the Community shall, for the purposes of this Chapter, be treated in the same way as natural persons who are nationals of member states.

'Companies or firms' means companies or firms constituted under civil or commercial law, including cooperative societies, and other legal persons governed by public or private law, save for those which are non-profit-making.

Article 59

Within the framework of the provisions set out below, restrictions on freedom to provide services within the Community shall be progressively abolished during the transitional period in respect of nationals of member states who are established in a state of the Community other than that of the person for whom the services are intended.

The Council may, acting unanimously on a proposal from the Commission, extend the provisions of this Chapter to nationals of a third country who provide services and who are established within the Community.

Article 60

Services shall be considered to be 'services' within the meaning of this Treaty where they are normally provided for remuneration, in so far as they are not governed by the provisions relating to freedom of movement for goods, capital and persons.

'Services' shall in particular include:

(a) activities of an industrial character;
(b) activities of a commercial character;
(c) activities of craftsmen;
(d) activities of the professions.

Without prejudice to the provisions of the Chapter relating to the right of establishment, the person providing a service may, in order to do so, temporarily pursue his activity in the state where the service is provided, under the same conditions as are imposed by that state on its own nationals.

Article 61

1. Freedom to provide services in the field of transport shall be governed by the provisions of the Title relating to transport.
2. The liberalisation of banking and insurance services connected with movements of capital shall be effected in step with the progressive liberalisation of movement of capital.

Article 62

Save as otherwise provided in this Treaty, member states shall not introduce any new restrictions on the freedom to provide services which have in fact been attained at the date of the entry into force of this Treaty.

Article 63

1. Before the end of the first stage, the Council shall, acting unanimously on a proposal from the Commission and after consulting the Economic and Social Committee and the Assembly, draw up a general programme for the abolition of existing restrictions on freedom to provide services within the Community. The Commission shall submit its proposal to the Council during the first two years of the first stage.

    The programme shall set out the general conditions under which and the stages by which each type of service is to be liberalised.

2. In order to implement this general programme or, in the absence of such programme, in order to achieve a stage in the liberalisation of a specific service, the Council shall, on a proposal from the Commission and after consulting the Economic and Social Committee and the Assembly, issue directives acting unanimously until the end of the first stage and by a qualified majority thereafter.

3. As regards the proposals and decisions referred to in paragraphs 1 and 2, priority shall as a general rule be given to those services which directly affect production costs or the liberalisation of which helps to promote trade in goods.

Article 64

The member states declare their readiness to undertake the liberalisation of services beyond the extent required by the directives issued pursuant to Article 63(2), if their general economic situation and the situation of the economic sector concerned so permit.

To this end, the Commission shall make recommendations to the member states concerned.

Article 65

As long as restrictions on freedom to provide services have not been abolished, each member state shall apply such restrictions without distinction on grounds of nationality or residence to all persons providing services within the meaning of the first paragraph of Article 59.

Article 66

The provisions of Articles 55 to 58 shall apply to the matters covered by this Chapter.

Company law harmonisation: list of Directives and Proposals

Legislation	Date adopted	Current position
First Directive (68/151) on the mandatory publication of specified company documents and information	1968	In force in all member states except Spain
Second Directive (77/91) dealing with the formation and capital of public companies	1976	In force in all member states except Spain
Third Directive (78/855) on mergers between two public companies subject to the laws of the same member state	1978	In force in all member states except Italy, Spain and Belgium
Fourth Directive (78/660) on annual accounts	1978	In force in all member states except Spain, Italy and Portugal. Implemented in the UK by the 1981 Companies Act
Proposal for a Fifth Company Law Directive on the structure of public limited companies and the powers and obligations of their organs		Amended proposal 1983
Sixth Directive (82/891) on the splitting up of public limited liability companies ('scissions')	1982	In force in all member states except Spain, Italy and Belgium. Scissions are not permitted in West Germany, Denmark or the Netherlands therefore this directive is not applicable in those member states.
Seventh Directive on consolidated accounts	1983	Partially implemented in member states

Legislation	Date adopted	Current position
Eighth Directive on the professional qualifications of statutory auditors	1984	Not yet implemented in the UK but currently in force in Belgium, Luxembourg, West Germany and Spain. The Directive will be implemented in the UK by the current Companies Bill
Proposal for a Ninth Directive on the conduct of groups containing a public limited company as a subsidiary		No formal proposal draft 1984
Draft Tenth Directive on international mergers of public companies		Current draft 1985
Draft Eleventh Directive on the disclosure requirements of branches of certain types of companies		Current draft COM 6346/89
Proposed Draft Twelfth Directive concerning single member private limited companies		Current draft COM 88/101
Proposed Directive on the information and consultation of workers in groups of companies (Vredeling Directive)		Amended draft 1983 withdrawn by the Commission. A revised proposal is being prepared by the Commission.
Directive on the accounts of banks	1986	The Directive must be implemented by 31 December 1990. In the UK, the DTI are preparing a consultative document on implementation
Regulation on the European Economic Interest Grouping	1985	Effective from 1 July 1989
Proposed regulation for a European Company Statute		Commission Memorandum 1988. Revised draft Statute expected early 1989

Legislation	Date adopted	Current position
Draft Proposed Directive on the accounts of insurance companies		Current position contained in Council Document 5468/89
Directive on the accounts of branches of banks	1989	In the UK implementation will take place at the same time as the Directive on the accounts of banks
Proposal for a Thirteenth Directive on takeovers and other general bids	1988	Current draft COM (88) 823
Proposed Directive on the accounts of certain partnerships		Current proposal 1988

Text of Articles 85 and 86 of the Treaty of Rome

Article 85

1. The following shall be prohibited as incompatible with the common market: all agreements between undertakings, decisions by associations of undertakings and concerted practices which may affect trade between member states and which have as their object or effect the prevention, restriction or distortion of competition within the common market, and in particular those which:

    (a) directly or indirectly fix purchase or selling prices or any other trading conditions;
    (b) limit or control production, markets, technical development, or investment;
    (c) share markets or sources of supply;
    (d) apply dissimilar conditions to equivalent transactions with other trading parties, thereby placing them at a competitive disadvantage;
    (e) make the conclusion of contracts subject to acceptance by the other parties of supplementary obligations which, by their nature or according to commercial usage, have no connection with the subject of such contracts.

2. Any agreements or decisions prohibited pursuant to this Article shall be automatically void.

3. The provisions of paragraph 1 may, however, be declared inapplicable in the case of:

    *   any agreement or category of agreements between undertakings;
    *   any decision or category of decisions by associations of undertakings;
    *   any concerted practice or category of concerted practices;

    which contributes to improving the production or distribution of goods or to promoting technical or economic progress, while allowing consumers a fair share of the resulting benefit, and which does not:

    (a) impose on the undertakings concerned restrictions which are not indispensable to the attainment of these objectives;
    (b) afford such undertakings the possibility of eliminating competition in respect of a substantial part of the products in question.

Article 86

Any abuse by one or more undertakings of a dominant position within the common market or in a substantial part of it shall be prohibited as incompatible with the common market in so far as it may affect trade between member states.

Such abuse may, in particular, consist in:

(a) directly or indirectly imposing unfair purchase or selling prices or other unfair trading conditions;

(b) limiting production, markets or technical development to the prejudice of consumers;

(c) applying dissimilar conditions to equivalent transactions with other trade parties, thereby placing them at a competitive disadvantage;

(d) making the conclusion of contracts subject to acceptance by the other parties of supplementary obligations which, by their nature or according to commercial usage, have no connection with the subject of such contracts.

Section 84 of the Fair Trading Act 1973: definition of 'Public Interest'

Public interest

1. In determining for any purposes to which this section applies whether any particular matter operates, or may be expected to operate, against the public interest, the Commission shall take into account all matters which appear to them in the particular circumstances to be relevant and, among other things, shall have regard to the desirability:

   (a) of maintaining and promoting effective competition between persons supplying goods and services in the United Kingdom;

   (b) of promoting the interests of consumers, purchasers and other users of goods and services in the United Kingdom in respect of the prices charged for them and in respect of their quality and the variety of goods and services supplied;

   (c) of promoting, through competition, the reduction of costs and the development and use of new techniques and new products, and of facilitating the entry of new competitors into existing markets;

(d) of maintaining and promoting the balanced distribution of industry and employment in the United Kingdom; and

(e) of maintaining and promoting competitive activity in markets outside the United Kingdom on the part of producers of goods, and of suppliers of goods and services, in the United Kingdom.

2. This section applies to the purpose of any functions of the Commission under this Act other than functions to which section 59(3) of this Act applies.

Tabulated summary of the laws, practices and 'culture' of selected member states in relation to international mergers

Country	General prohibition on international acquisitions	Sectoral prohibitions	Corporate shareholding, cultural factors, etc.
Belgium	Finance Minister can block public takeover bids by investors from non-EC companies. (Draft legislation when enacted will force shareholders with more than 10 per cent to disclose their interest.) Prior authorisation required for foreign investment in particular sectors.	• Maritime transport • Insurance (non-EC member companies may be subject to reciprocity requirements) *Public monopolies:* • Air transport • Telephone, telegraph and postal services • Inland waterways and ports • Radio and TV broadcasting • Water distribution	Transfer of one third of equity or more of large companies must be notified in advance to Government. Any public bid is subject to the Belgium Banking Commission's prior review. A prospectus must be submitted to the Banking Commission together with a detailed file that should include justification as to price. *Rules to note:* 1. Once the BC decides that control has passed, an obligatory offer must be made to all shareholders. 2. In a rare hostile situation, counterbids must be made at a level constituting a certain percentage increase on the bid price. Nationalistic reaction to Suchard's takeover of Côte d'Or (1987). Similar antipathy to de Bendetti's assault on Société Générale.

France	See pp. 166–82. Non-EC nationals need prior authorisation from Finance Ministry to take more than 20 per cent of a French company. Prior authorisation required for certain investments (including those involving activities concerned with public order, public health and national security). Acquisitions can also be referred to the Competition Council.	Special measures apply, or govern more strictly, non-residents in certain sectors, including merchants and craftsmen; exploration and exploitation of mines, quarries and waterfalls; oil; the nuclear industry; transportation; agriculture; insurance; banking. *Public Monopolies:* ● Gunpowder and explosives ● Tobacco and matches ● Postal services ● Telecommunication and TV ● Electricity	Since October 1987 previously liberal attitude to both foreign and domestic takeovers hardening. Corporate defences have increased, as have Government disclosure requirements. In privatised companies 'hard cores' of friendly shareholders are banned from selling for two years.
Italy	See pp. 166–82.	Limited reservations apply to foreign majority participation in companies in the information sector; owning aircraft; owning certain Italian ships. Establishment of branches of banks from non-EC member states is subject to a minimum capital requirement. Special measures apply to non-resident investors in maritime and air transport; banking; insurance. *Public monopolies:* ● Postal services and telecommunications ● Electricity, gas, water and nuclear energy ● Railways ● Local community public services ● RAI TV broadcasts at national level	Potential large-scale corporate takeovers tend to undergo political scrutiny. Big groups (e.g. Fiat, Pirelli) have reorganised the ultimate family holding companies which control their industrial empires, using such devices as minority equity stakes, to form a limited partnership of trust, making hostile takeovers extremely difficult.

continued overleaf

Country	General prohibition on international acquisitions	Sectoral prohibitions	Corporate shareholding, cultural factors, etc.
Netherlands	No laws forbid foreign acquisitions, they are governed (as domestic ones) by the Merger Code of the Social Economic Council (a body representing unions, employers and Government, but with no sanction powers). Under the code, unions must be informed of bids but have no statutory powers to block takeovers. The Code's rules are aimed at protecting the interests of shareholders and employers, and prescribe notification of proposed mergers with the Government.	Special measures apply to foreign investment in maritime and air transport; banking; armaments; insurance. *Public monopolies:* • Telecommunications and postal services • Railways • Regional electricity companies *Privately operated or mixed monopolies:* • Broadcasting • Public bus transport	Dutch companies build in permanent structures, e.g. *structuur vennootschap* – a form of incorporation where the management has far-ranging powers to run the company. The use of priority shares and pre-ferred shares, the latter being issued at the board's discretion, are common, specifically, to avoid takeovers.
Spain	See pp. 166–82. Recent formal and informal restrictions have been reimposed on foreign bank takeovers and acquisitions in response to the aggressive attitude taken by foreign companies when restrictions were originally lifted eight years ago. A reciprocity requirement is now imposed.	Limited reservation applies to investment exceeding 25 per cent of the equity in public utilities and air trans-port companies as well as certain per-centages of shareholdings in companies in maritime transport; mining; oil refining; banks; broadcast-ing telecommunications; water resources. Casinos and insurance are also subject to special restrictions.	Trade unions have no power to block takeovers and do not have to be con-sulted. Although they have been active lobbyists (e.g. in relation to the stakes acquired by the Kuwait Investment Office in the Ebro sugar concern and the chemical company Union Explo-sives Rio-Tinto). Political attitudes very liberal, although Finance Ministry would prefer foreign companies to use their purchases as core business from which to attach European markets and not just as marginal affiliates.

continued overleaf

Spain (cont.)	In relation to EC member states, Spain together with Portugal has had an extension to the period for liberalisation of free movement of capital under the 1992 programme. This may be extended further if they have difficulties making the deadline.	*Public monopolies:* • Railways • Telegraph, telephone and postal services • TV • Nuclear industries *Private monopolies:* • Sale of duty free goods *Mixed monopolies:* • Distribution of petroleum products • Tobacco • Certain categories of insurance	
UK	Industry Act 1975 gives Government the power to prevent 'foreign control of important undertakings in manufacturing industry which would be contrary to the national interest' – in practice this power has never been used. If used against an EC company it would probably be challenged as contrary to the EC Treaty. Takeover bids or the substantial acquisition of states in companies can be referred for investigation by the Government to the Monopolies and Mergers Commission.	Banking Act gives the Bank of England wide powers to decide what is a 'fit and proper' investor in a bank, and the Governor of the Bank of England has indicated that approval is unlikely to be given to the foreign takeover of a clearing bank. Special measures apply to non-resident investors in maritime transport; broadcasting; insurance.	General *laissez faire* attitude to competition and free market. The Government has referred the Kuwait Investment Office shareholding in BP to the MMC (with a recommendation that it be reduced to 9.9 per cent) and has previously prevented the takeover of the Royal Bank of Scotland by the Hong Kong and Shanghai Bank.

continued overleaf

Country	General prohibition on international acquisitions	Sectoral prohibitions	Corporate shareholding, cultural factors, etc.
UK (cont.)		*Public monopolies:* ● Postal services ● Rail ● Water distribution ● Gas supply *Privately operated or mixed monopolies:* ● Coal production ● Telecommunications	
West Germany	See pp. 166–82.	Special measures apply to non-resident investors in air and maritime transport; banking. *Public monopolies:* ● Telegraph, telephone and certain postal services ● Roads and motorways ● Railways ● Inland waterways and ports ● Telecommunications ● Airports ● Lotteries ● Radio and TV broadcasting	The Cartel law can sometimes make it easier for a foreign company not already involved in West Germany to make an acquisition rather than a domestic one. Some West German companies have taken steps to limit voting rights to avoid takeovers from abroad. There are very few listed publicly owned West German companies and most of their equity is controlled by the banks. As a result, there were no successful hostile bids in 1987.

Appendix II: Further reading and reference

S J Berwin & Co, *The 1988 Businessman's Guide to EEC Legal Developments*, 1988. Volume 1, *1992: The New Business Environment*; Volume 2, *Intellectual Property and Competition*. The first volume is a study of *inter alia* the single market, with particular reference to the free movement of goods, public tendering and procurement, consumer protection, financial services, capital movements, fiscal harmonisation, company law and telecommunications. The second volume includes sections on competition, including treatment of joint ventures, merger control and block exemptions.

EUROPE 1992: Developing an Active Company Approach to the European Market, 1988, Commission of the European Communities.

Europe without Frontiers: Completing the Internal Market, 2nd ed., 1988, European Documentation, Office for Official Publications, 2985 Luxembourg.

P.S.R.F. Mathijsen, *A Guide to European Community Law*, Sweet & Maxwell, 1985. This is an introductory book on the institutions and law of the EC; it is written in simple concise terms and suitable for non-specialist readers.

Emile Noël, *Working Together: The Institutions of the European Community*, Office of Official Publications of the European Communities, 1988. Outlines the function of the principal Community Institutions and their respective roles in the decision-making process.

Rudden and Wyatt (eds.), *Basic Community Laws*, Oxford University Press, 1986. This collection of Treaty material and secondary legislation includes the text of the Treaty of Rome as amended by the Single European Act, and the major EC regulations on Competition law.

The following brochures for businesses, published by the Office for Official Publications, may be obtained from the regional Community information offices: *Public Supply Contracts in the European Community; EEC Competition Rules: Guide for Small and Medium-Sized Enterprises; The European Commission's Powers of Investigation in the Enforcement of Competition Law*

Index